First and Second Things

C.S. Lewis is renowned as an author of many books on Christianity, as well as for a science fiction trilogy, *The Chronicles of Narnia* and many works of literary criticism.

He was born in Ireland in 1898, gained a Triple First at Oxford and was Fellow and Tutor at Magdalen College 1925–54, when he became Professor of Medieval and Renaissance English Literature at Cambridge. He died in November 1963, at his home in Oxford.

Walter Hooper was born in Reidsville, North Carolina, in 1931. He read theology and then lectured on Medieval and Renaissance English at the University of Kentucky.

In 1963 he became companion-secretary to C.S. Lewis, a post he filled for the remaining months of the Professor's life. Still resident in Oxford, Father Hooper is the Literary Adviser to the C.S. Lewis Estate and a recognized authority on the Professor's works.

Available in Fount Paperbacks by C. S. Lewis

The Abolition of Man
The Business of Heaven
Christian Reflections
The Dark Tower
Fern-seed and Elephants
The Four Loves
God in the Dock
The Great Divorce
Letters
Letters to Children
Letters to Malcolm: Chiefly on Prayer
Mere Christianity
Miracles
Of This and Other Worlds
The Pilgrim's Regress
Present Concerns
The Problem of Pain
Reflections on the Psalms
The Screwtape Letters
Screwtape Proposes a Toast, and Other Pieces
Surprised by Joy
Till We Have Faces
Timeless at Heart

Available as Lions

The Chronicles of Narnia

First and Second Things

Essays on Theology and Ethics

C.S. LEWIS

Edited by Walter Hooper

Collins
FOUNT PAPERBACKS

First published in *Undeceptions*
by Geoffrey Bles, London 1971
This edition first published in Great Britain
in 1985 by Fount Paperbacks
Second impression January 1989

Copyright © 1985 C. S. Lewis Pte. Ltd

Printed and bound in Great Britain by
William Collins Sons & Co. Ltd, Glasgow

Contents

Preface

On 26th October 1769 Boswell said to Dr Johnson, "If, Sir, you were shut up in a castle, and a new-born child with you, what would you do?" "Why, Sir," replied Dr Johnson, "I should not much like my company." Boswell, however, persevered with his questions about the rearing of the child until Dr Johnson said with some heat, "Sir, I would not *coddle* the child."

Dr Johnson was so worth listening to on almost any subject that it was inevitable that he be asked some very odd questions. C.S. Lewis told me he was grateful no one had ever asked him what he'd do with a baby. Still, I doubt if many people since Dr Johnson have had their advice sought so often and on so many subjects as Lewis. It is unfortunate that there was no Boswell to record his conversation, but we are fortunate that he wrote on such a variety of topics. On the other hand, I am one of those to whom Lewis sometimes said, "I don't know enough to have an opinion about that." When he believed himself to be too ignorant to write on some of the things he was asked about he told his correspondents "the cow is milked dry" or "the teapot is watered till it's no good calling it tea" or "the pump-handle is beginning to creak". But, like Dr Johnson, if Lewis had an informed opinion about something he thought he should write on he took pains to do it well.

Because I have edited other works of Lewis's, a great many people write to me asking what Lewis thought about Religious Education in schools, capital punishment, the commercialization of Christmas and many other things. Those who write usually express their disappointment and even fury with those bishops and clergymen so theologically "broad" that there is no sense to be had from them. And, really, it is difficult to understand how these clerics could reach middle age and not have discovered the truth of Dean W.R. Inge's warning that "He who marries the Spirit of the Age will soon be a widower." What, ask those who write to me, did *Lewis*, with his unwavering certitude about the Christian Faith, believe about various subjects? I have needed to explain – as I do here – that many of Lewis's finest essays were published under the title *Undeceptions: Essays on Theology and Ethics* (1971) and that the recession has made it unwise to reprint that large book. One Fount Paperback, *God in the Dock*, consists of selections from *Undeceptions*. This is another selection from the parent book and it contains essays on Religious Education in schools and the other topics mentioned above.

With one notable exception – "The Humanitarian Theory of Punishment" – I think the essays in this collection were written at the request of those who asked for something from Lewis's pen. I am grateful to all those publishers who first allowed me to reprint them in *Undeceptions*. I acknowledge their permission again by supplying the original sources of the essays which make up *First and Second Things*.

(1) "Bulverism or, The Foundation of Twentieth-century Thought" is Lewis's title for the essay which appeared as "Notes on the Way" in *Time and Tide*, Vol. XXII (29th March 1941) p. 261.

(2) "First and Second Things" is the name Lewis gave this essay which first appeared as "Notes on the Way" in *Time and Tide*, Vol. XXIII (27th June 1942) pp. 519–20.

(3) "On the Reading of Old Books" is my title for Lewis's Preface to St Athanasius's *The Incarnation of the Word of God*, translated by A Religious of C.S.M.V., first published by Geoffrey Bles Ltd in 1944 and by A.R. Mowbray and Co. Ltd in 1953.

(4) "Horrid Red Things" was originally published in the *Church of England Newspaper*, Vol. LI (6th October 1944) pp. 1–2.

(5) "Work and Prayer" first appeared in *The Coventry Evening Telegraph* (28th May 1945) p. 4.

(6) "Two Lectures" is Lewis's title for an essay originally published as "Who was Right – Dream Lecturer or Real Lecturer?" in *The Coventry Evening Telegraph* (21st February 1945) p. 4.

(7) "Meditation in a Toolshed" is reprinted from *The Coventry Evening Telegraph* (17th July 1945) p. 4.

(8) "The Sermon and the Lunch" is reprinted from the *Church of England Newspaper*, No. 2692 (21st September 1945) pp. 1–2.

(9) "On the Transmission of Christianity", which is primarily about Religious Education in schools, is my title for Lewis's Preface to G.B. Sandhurst's *How Heathen is Britain?* (Collins, 1946).

(10) "The Decline of Religion" is taken from an

Oxford periodical, *The Cherwell*, Vol. XXVI (29th November 1946) pp. 8–10.

(11) "Vivisection" appeared first as a pamphlet from the New England Anti-Vivisection Society (1947) and it was reprinted in this country by the National Anti-Vivisection Society (1948).

(12) "Modern Translations of the Bible" is my title for Lewis's Preface to J.B. Phillips's *Letters to Young Churches: A Translation of the New Testament Epistles* (Geoffrey Bles Ltd, 1947).

(13) "Some Thoughts" was written at the request of the Medical Missionaries of Mary who founded Our Lady of Lourdes Hospital at Drogheda, Ireland, and it was published in *The First Decade: Ten Years' Work of the Medical Missionaries of Mary* (Dublin: At the Sign of the Three Candles, 1948) pp. 91–4.

(14) I do not know which English publishers Lewis sent "The Humanitarian Theory of Punishment" to. It was first published in *20th Century: An Australian Quarterly Review*, Vol. III, No. 3 (1949) pp. 5–12. At the end of the essay Lewis added this postscript: "One last word. You may ask why I send this to an Australian periodical. The reason is simple and perhaps worth recording: I can get no hearing for it in England." The essay found a serious hearing in Australia and two criminologists, Norval Morris and Donald Buckle, published "A Reply to C.S. Lewis" in *20th Century*, Vol. VI, No. 2 (1952). After this Lewis's essay and Drs Morris and Buckle's "Reply" were reprinted in the Australian law journal *Res Judicatae*, Vol. VI (June 1953) pp. 224–30 and pp. 231–7. Then came J.J.C. Smart's "Comment: The Humanitarian Theory of Punishment"

in *Res Judicatae*, Vol. VI (February 1954). This caused Lewis to write "On Punishment: A Reply" – a reply to all three men – which was published in *Res Judicatae*, Vol. VI (August 1954) pp. 519–23. Later, when Lewis allowed the English journal, *The Modern Churchman*, to reprint his original essay, he removed the postscript. It has since been reprinted in a number of American collections of essays on capital punishment and related issues. Of all Lewis's essays this is one of the most respected and certainly the most controversial. This book contains the original essay as well as Lewis's "On Punishment: A Reply".

(15) "Xmas and Christmas: A Lost Chapter from Herodotus" was first published in *Time and Tide*, Vol. XXXV (4th December 1954) p. 1607.

(16) "Revival or Decay?" is reprinted from *Punch*, Vol. CCXXV (9th July 1858) pp. 36–8.

(17) "Before We Can Communicate" was originally published in *Breakthrough*, No. 8 (October 1961) p. 2.

It should be mentioned that all the footnotes are mine except number 1 on page 108, number 2 on page 109, and numbers 1 and 2 on page 112, which are Lewis's.

As I said, C.S. Lewis was glad no one asked him how he'd rear a baby in a castle, and we laughed at that incident recorded in Boswell's *Life of Johnson*. I think it was because Lewis thought I *was* planning to ask him the same question (I was) that he said to me: "What would you do if you were shut up in a castle with a liberal theologian anxious to explain away the Resurrection, the Incarnation and the Virgin Birth?" "I'm sure", I replied, "that I would go mad." "No need for that", said Lewis. "Whenever you have to listen to a liberal theologian explain why you can't believe in some doctrine of the Faith ask him the moment he's finished to repeat what he's said. You'll find he won't be able to say the same thing a second time without even greater confusion." I've never been shut up in a castle with a liberal theologian, but I've asked many to repeat what they have just said. Lewis was right – exact repetition of nonsense is impossible. The essays published here are proof that Lewis never married the Spirit of the Age. He never even flirted with her.

28th January 1985   Walter Hooper
Oxford

1

Bulverism
or, The Foundation of
Twentieth-century Thought

(*1941*)

It is a disastrous discovery, as Emerson says somewhere, that we exist. I mean, it is disastrous when instead of merely attending to a rose we are forced to think of ourselves looking at the rose, with a certain type of mind and a certain type of eyes. It is disastrous because, if you are not very careful, the colour of the rose gets attributed to our optic nerves and its scent to our noses, and in the end there is no rose left. The professional philosophers have been bothered about this universal black-out for over two hundred years, and the world has not much listened to them. But the same disaster is now occurring on a level we can all understand.

We have recently "discovered that we exist" in two new senses. The Freudians have discovered that we exist as bundles of complexes. The Marxians have discovered that we exist as members of some economic class. In the old days it was supposed that if a thing seemed obviously true to a hundred men, then it was probably true in fact. Nowadays the Freudian will tell you to go and analyse the hundred: you will find that they all think Elizabeth [I] a great queen because they all have a mother-complex. Their thoughts are psychologically tainted at the source. And the Marxist will tell you to go and examine the economic interests of the hundred; you will find that they all think freedom a good thing because they are all members of the bourgeoisie whose prosperity is increased by a policy of *laissez-faire*. Their thoughts are "ideologically tainted" at the source.

Now this is obviously great fun; but it has not always been noticed that there is a bill to pay for it. There are two questions that people who say this kind of thing ought to be asked. The first is, Are *all* thoughts thus tainted at the source, or only some? The second is, Does the taint invalidate the tainted thought – in the sense of making it untrue – or not?

If they say that *all* thoughts are thus tainted, then, of course, we must remind them that Freudianism and Marxism are as much systems of thought as Christian theology or philosophical idealism. The Freudian and the Marxian are in the same boat with all the rest of us, and cannot criticize us from outside. They have sawn off the branch they were sitting on. If, on the other hand, they say that the taint need not invalidate their thinking, then neither need it invalidate ours. In which case they have saved their own branch, but also saved ours along with it.

The only line they can really take is to say that some thoughts are tainted and others are not – which has the advantage (if Freudians and Marxians regard it as an advantage) of being what every sane man has always believed. But if that is so, we must then ask how you find out which are tainted and which are not. It is no earthly use saying that those are tainted which agree with the secret wishes of the thinker. *Some* of the things I should like to believe must in fact be true; it is impossible to arrange a universe which contradicts everyone's wishes, in every respect, at every moment. Suppose I think, after doing my accounts, that I have a large balance at the bank. And suppose you want to find out whether this belief of mine is "wishful thinking". You can never come to any conclusion by examining my psychological condition. Your only chance of finding out is to sit down and work through the sum yourself. When you have checked my figures, then, and then only, will you know whether I have that balance or not. If you find my arithmetic correct, then no amount of vapouring about my psychological condition can be anything but a waste of time. If you find my arithmetic wrong, then it may be relevant to explain psychologically how I came to be so bad at my arithmetic, and the doctrine of the concealed wish will become relevant – but only *after* you have yourself done the sum and discovered me to be wrong on purely arithmetical grounds. It is the same with all thinking and all systems of thought. If you try to find out which are tainted by speculating about the wishes of the thinkers, you are merely making a fool of yourself. You must find out on purely logical grounds which of them do, in fact, break down as arguments. Afterwards, if you like, go on and discover the psychological causes of the error.

In other words, you must show *that* a man is wrong before you start explaining *why* he is wrong. The modern method is to assume without discussion *that* he is wrong and then distract his attention from this (the only real issue) by busily explaining how he became so silly. In the course of the last fifteen years I have found this vice so common that I have had to invent a name for it. I

call it Bulverism. Some day I am going to write the
biography of its imaginary inventor, Ezekiel Bulver,
whose destiny was determined at the age of five when he
heard his mother say to his father – who had been
maintaining that two sides of a triangle were together
greater than the third – "Oh, you say that *because you are
a man*." "At that moment", E. Bulver assures us, "there
flashed across my opening mind the great truth that
refutation is no necessary part of argument. Assume that
your opponent is wrong, and then explain his error, and
the world will be at your feet. Attempt to prove that he is
wrong or (worse still) try to find out whether he is wrong
or right, and the national dynamism of our age will
thrust you to the wall." That is how Bulver became one
of the makers of the Twentieth Century.

I find the fruits of his discovery almost everywhere.
Thus I see my religion dismissed on the grounds that
"the comfortable parson had every reason for assuring
the nineteenth-century worker that poverty would be
rewarded in another world". Well, no doubt he had. On
the assumption that Christianity is an error, I can see
easily enough that some people would still have a motive
for inculcating it. I see it so easily that I can, of course,
play the game the other way round, by saying that "the
modern man has every reason for trying to convince
himself that there are no eternal sanctions behind the
morality he is rejecting". For Bulverism is a truly demo-
cratic game in the sense that all can play it all day long,
and that it gives no unfair privilege to the small and
offensive minority who reason. But of course it gets us
not one inch nearer to deciding whether, as a matter of
fact, the Christian religion is true or false. That question

remains to be discussed on quite different grounds – a matter of philosophical and historical argument. However it were decided, the improper motives of some people, both for believing it and for disbelieving it, would remain just as they are.

I see Bulverism at work in every political argument. The capitalists must be bad economists because we know why they want capitalism, and equally the Communists must be bad economists because we know why they want Communism. Thus, the Bulverists on both sides. In reality, of course, either the doctrines of the capitalists are false, or the doctrines of the Communists, or both; but you can only find out the rights and wrongs by reasoning – never by being rude about your opponent's psychology.

Until Bulverism is crushed, reason can play no effective part in human affairs. Each side snatches it early as a weapon against the other; but between the two reason itself is discredited. And why should reason not be discredited? It would be easy, in answer, to point to the present state of the world, but the real answer is even more immediate. The forces discrediting reason, themselves depend on reasoning. You must reason even to Bulverize. You are trying to *prove* that all *proofs* are invalid. If you fail, you fail. If you succeed, then you fail even more – for the proof that all proofs are invalid must be invalid itself.

The alternative then is either sheer self-contradicting idiocy or else some tenacious belief in our power of reasoning, held in the teeth of all the evidence that Bulverists can bring for a "taint" in this or that human reasoner. I am ready to admit, if you like, that this tenacious belief has something transcendental or mystical about it. What then? Would you rather be a lunatic than a mystic?

So we see there is justification for holding on to our belief in Reason. But can this be done without theism? Does "I know" involve that God exists? Everything I know is an inference from sensation (except the present moment). All our knowledge of the universe beyond our immediate experiences depends on inferences from these experiences. If our inferences do not give a genuine insight into reality, then we can know nothing. A theory cannot be accepted if it does not allow our thinking to be a genuine insight, nor if the fact of our knowledge is not explicable in terms of that theory.

But our thoughts can only be accepted as a genuine insight under certain conditions. All beliefs have causes but a distinction must be drawn between (1) ordinary causes and (2) a special kind of cause called "a reason". Causes are mindless events which can produce other results than belief. Reasons arise from axioms and inferences and affect only beliefs. Bulverism tries to show that the other man has causes and not reasons and that we have reasons and not causes. A belief which can be accounted for entirely in terms of causes is worthless. This principle must not be abandoned when we consider the beliefs which are the basis of others. Our knowledge depends on our certainty about axioms and inferences. If these are the result of causes, then there is no possibility of knowledge. Either we can know nothing *or* thought has reasons only, and no causes.

2

First and Second Things

(*1942*)

When I read in *Time and Tide* on 6th June [1942] that the Germans have selected Hagen in preference to Siegfried as their national hero, I could have laughed out loud for pleasure. For I am a romantic person who has frankly revelled in my Nibelungs, and specially in Wagner's version of the story, ever since one golden summer in adolescence when I first heard the "Ride of the Valkyries" on a gramophone and saw Arthur Rackham's illustrations to *The Ring*. Even now the very smell of those volumes can come over me with the poignancy of remembered calf-love. It was, therefore, a bitter moment when the Nazis took over my treasure and made it part of their ideology. But now all is well. They have proved unable to digest it. They can retain it only by standing the story on its head and making one of the minor villains the hero. Doubtless the logic of their position will presently drive them further, and Alberich will be announced as the true personification of the Nordic spirit. In the meantime, they have given me back what they stole.

The mention of the Nordic spirit reminds me that their attempted appropriation of *The Ring* is only one instance of their larger attempt to appropriate "the Nordic" as a whole, and this larger attempt is equally ridiculous. What business have people who call might right to say they are worshippers of Odin? The whole point about Odin was that he had the right but not the might. The whole point about Norse religion was that it alone of all mythologies told men to serve gods who were admittedly fighting with their backs to the wall and would certainly be defeated in the end. "I am off to die with Odin" said the rover in Stevenson's fable,[1] thus proving that Stevenson understood something about the Nordic spirit which Germany has never been able to understand at all. The gods will fall. The wisdom of Odin, the humorous courage of Thor (Thor was something of a Yorkshireman) and the beauty of Balder will all be smashed eventually by the *Realpolitik* of the stupid giants and misshapen trolls. But that does not in the least alter the allegiance of any free man. Hence, as we should expect, real Germanic poetry is all about heroic stands, and fighting against hopeless odds.

At this stage it occurred to me that I had stumbled on a rather remarkable paradox. How is it that the only people in Europe who have tried to revive their pre-Christian mythology as a living faith should also be the people that shows itself incapable of understanding that mythology in its very rudiments? The retrogression would, in any case, be deplorable – just as it would be deplorable if a full grown man reverted to the *ethos* of his preparatory school. But you would expect him at least to get the no-sneaking rule right, and to be quite clear that new boys ought not to put their hands in their pockets.

[1] This is found in R.L. Stevenson's "Faith, Half-Faith, and No Faith", first published in *The Strange Case of Dr Jekyll and Mr Hyde with other Fables* (London, 1896).

To sacrifice the greater good for the less and then not to get the lesser good after all – that is the surprising folly. To sell one's birthright for a mess of mythology and then to get the mythology all wrong – how did they do it? For it is quite clear that I (who would rather paint my face bright blue with woad than suggest that there is a real Odin) am actually getting out of Odin all the good and all the fun that Odin can supply, while the Nazi Odinists are getting none of it.

And yet, it seemed to me as I thought about it, this may not be such a paradox as it looks. Or, at least, it is a paradox which turns up so often that a man ought by now to be accustomed to it. Other instances began to come to mind. Until quite modern times – I think, until the time of the Romantics – nobody ever suggested that literature and the arts were an end in themselves. They "belonged to the ornamental part of life", they provided "innocent diversion"; or else they "refined our manners" or "incited us to virtue" or glorified the gods. The great music had been written for Masses, the great pictures painted to fill up a space on the wall of a noble patron's dining-room or to kindle devotion in a church; the great tragedies were produced either by religious poets in honour of Dionysus or by commercial poets to entertain Londoners on half-holidays. It was only in the nineteenth century that we became aware of the full dignity of art. We began to "take it seriously" as the Nazis take mythology seriously. But the result seems to have been a dislocation of the aesthetic life in which little is left us but high-minded works which fewer and fewer people want to read or hear or see, and "popular" works of which both those who make them and those who enjoy them are half ashamed. Just like the Nazis, by valuing too highly a real, but subordinate good, we have come near to losing that good itself.

The longer I looked into it the more I came to suspect that I was perceiving a universal law. *On cause mieux quand on ne dit pas Causons.*[1] The woman who makes a dog the centre of her life loses, in the end, not only her human usefulness and dignity but even the proper pleasure of dog-keeping. The man who makes alcohol his chief good loses not only his job but his palate and all power of enjoying the earlier (and only pleasurable) levels of intoxication. It is a glorious thing to feel for a moment or two that the whole meaning of the universe is summed up in one woman – glorious so long as other duties and pleasures keep tearing you away from her. But clear the decks and so arrange your life (it is sometimes feasible) that you will have nothing to do but contemplate her, and what happens? Of course this law has been discovered before, but it will stand re-discovery. It may be stated as follows: every prefer-ence of a small good to a great, or a partial good to a total good, involves the loss of the small or partial good for which the sacrifice was made.

Apparently the world is made that way. If Esau really got the pottage in return for his birthright,[2] then Esau was a lucky exception. You can't get second things by putting them first; you can get second things only by putting first things first. From which it would follow that the question, "What things are first?", is of concern not only to philosophers but to everyone.

[1] One converses better when one does not say "Let us converse".
[2] Genesis 25.

It is impossible, in this context, not to inquire what our own civilization has been putting first for the last thirty years. And the answer is plain. It has been putting itself first. To preserve civilization has been the great aim; the collapse of civilization, the great bugbear. Peace, a high standard of life, hygiene, transport, science and amusement – all these, which are what we usually mean by civilization, have been our ends. It will be replied that our concern for civilization is very natural and very necessary at a time when civilization is so imperilled. But how if the shoe is on the other foot? – how if civilization has been imperilled precisely by the fact that we have all made civilization our *summum bonum*? Perhaps it can't be preserved in that way. Perhaps civilization will never be safe until we care for something else more than we care for it.

The hypothesis has certain facts to support it. As far as peace (which is one ingredient in our idea of civilization) is concerned, I think many would now agree that a foreign policy dominated by desire for peace is one of the many roads that lead to war. And was civilization ever seriously endangered until civilization became the exclusive aim of human activity? There is much rash idealization of past ages about, and I do not wish to encourage more of it. Our ancestors were cruel, lecherous, greedy and stupid, like ourselves. But while they cared for other things more than for civilization – and they cared at different times for all sorts of things, for the will of God, for glory, for personal honour, for doctrinal purity, for justice – was civilization often in serious danger of disappearing?

At least the suggestion is worth a thought. To be sure,

if it were true that civilization will never be safe till it is put second, that immediately raises the question, second to what? What is the first thing? The only reply I can offer here is that if we do not know, then the first, and only truly practical thing, is to set about finding out.

3

On the Reading
of Old Books
(*1944*)

There is a strange idea abroad that in every subject the ancient books should be read only by the professionals, and that the amateur should content himself with the modern books. Thus I have found as a tutor in English Literature that if the average student wants to find out something about Platonism, the very last thing he thinks of doing is to take a translation of Plato off the library shelf and read the *Symposium*. He would rather read some dreary modern book ten times as long, all about "isms" and influences and only once in twelve pages telling him what Plato actually said. The error is rather an amiable one, for it springs from humility. The student is half afraid to meet one of the great philosophers face to face. He feels himself inadequate and thinks he will not understand him. But if he only knew, the great man, just because of his greatness, is much more intelligible than his modern commentator. The simplest student will be able to understand, if not all, yet a very great deal of what Plato said; but hardly anyone can understand some modern books on Platonism. It has always therefore been one of my main endeavours as a teacher to persuade the young that first-hand knowledge is not only more worth acquiring than second-hand knowledge, but is usually much easier and more delightful to acquire.

This mistaken preference for the modern books and this shyness of the old ones is nowhere more rampant than in theology. Wherever you find a little study circle of Christian laity you can be almost certain that they are studying not St Luke or St Paul or St Augustine or Thomas Aquinas or Hooker or Butler, but M. Berdyaev or M. Maritain or Mr Niebuhr or Miss Sayers or even myself.

Now this seems to me topsy-turvy. Naturally, since I myself am a writer, I do not wish the ordinary reader to read no modern books. But if he must read only the new or only the old, I would advise him to read the old. And I would give him this advice precisely because he is an amateur and therefore much less protected than the expert against the dangers of an exclusive contemporary diet. A new book is still on its trial and the amateur is not in a position to judge it. It has to be tested against the great body of Christian thought down the ages, and all its hidden implications (often unsuspected by the author himself) have to be brought to light. Often it cannot be fully understood without the knowledge of a good many other modern books. If you join at eleven o'clock a conversation which began at eight you will often not see the real bearing of what is said. Remarks which seem to you very ordinary will produce laughter or irritation and you will not see why – the reason, of course, being that the earlier stages of the conversation have given them a special point. In the same way sentences in a modern book which look quite ordinary may be directed "at" some other book; in this way you may be led to accept what you would have indignantly rejected if you knew its real significance. The only safety is to have a standard of plain, central Christianity ("mere Christianity" as Baxter called it) which puts the controversies of the moment in their proper perspective. Such a standard can be acquired only from the old books. It is a good rule, after reading a new book, never to allow yourself another new one till you have read an old one in between. If that is too much for you, you should at least read one old one to every three new ones.

Every age has its own outlook. It is specially good at seeing certain truths and specially liable to make certain mistakes. We all, therefore, need the books that will correct the characteristic mistakes of our own period. And that means the old books. All contemporary writers share to some extent the contemporary outlook – even those, like myself, who seem most opposed to it. Nothing strikes me more when I read the controversies of past ages than the fact that both sides were usually assuming without question a good deal which we should now absolutely deny. They thought that they were as completely opposed as two sides could be, but in fact they were all the time secretly united – united *with* each other and *against* earlier and later ages – by a great mass of common assumptions. We may be sure that the characteristic blindness of the twentieth century – the blindness about which posterity will ask, "But how *could* they have thought that?" – lies where we have never suspected it, and concerns something about which there is untroubled agreement between Hitler and President Roosevelt[1] or between Mr H.G. Wells and Karl Barth.

[1] This was written in 1943.

None of us can fully escape this blindness, but we shall certainly increase it, and weaken our guard against it, if we read only modern books. Where they are true they will give us truths which we half knew already. Where they are false they will aggravate the error with which we are already dangerously ill. The only palliative is to keep the clean sea breeze of the centuries blowing through our minds, and this can be done only by reading old books. Not, of course, that there is any magic about the past. People were no cleverer then than they are now; they made as many mistakes as we. But not the *same* mistakes. They will not flatter us in the errors we are already committing; and their own errors, being now open and palpable, will not endanger us. Two heads are better than one, not because either is infallible, but because they are unlikely to go wrong in the same direction. To be sure, the books of the future would be just as good a corrective as the books of the past, but unfortunately we cannot get at them.

I myself was first led into reading the Christian classics, almost accidentally, as a result of my English studies. Some, such as Hooker, Herbert, Traherne, Taylor and Bunyan, I read because they are themselves great English writers; others, such as Boethius,[1] St Augustine, Thomas Aquinas and Dante, because they were "influences". George MacDonald I had found for myself at the age of sixteen and never wavered in my allegiance, though I tried for a long time to ignore his Christianity. They are, you will note, a mixed bag, representative of many Churches, climates and ages. And

[1] Boethius was born about A.D. 470 and wrote *The Consolation of Philosophy*.

that brings me to yet another reason for reading them. The divisions of Christendom are undeniable and are by some of these writers most fiercely expressed. But if any man is tempted to think – as one might be tempted who read only contemporaries – that "Christianity" is a word of so many meanings that it means nothing at all, he can learn beyond all doubt, by stepping out of his own century, that this is not so. Measured against the ages "mere Christianity" turns out to be no insipid interdenominational transparency, but something positive, self-consistent, and inexhaustible. I know it, indeed, to my cost. In the days when I still hated Christianity,[1] I learned to recognize, like some all too familiar smell, that almost unvarying *something* which met me, now in Puritan Bunyan, now in Anglican Hooker, now in Thomist Dante. It was there (honeyed and floral) in François de Sales; it was there (grave and homely) in Spenser and Walton; it was there (grim but manful) in Pascal and Johnson; there again, with a mild, frightening, Paradisial flavour, in Vaughan and Boehme and Traherne. In the urban sobriety of the eighteenth century one was not safe – Law and Butler were two lions in the path. The supposed "Paganism" of the Elizabethans could not keep it out; it lay in wait where a man might have supposed himself safest, in the very centre of *The Faerie Queene* and the *Arcadia*.[2] It was, of course, varied; and yet – after all – so unmistakably the same; recognizable, not to be evaded, the odour which is death to us until we allow it to become life:

---

[1] Those who wish to know more about this period should read Lewis's autobiography, *Surprised by Joy: The Shape of My Early Life* (London, 1955).
[2] By Sir Philip Sydney (1554–86).

an air that kills
From yon far country blows.[1]

We are all rightly distressed, and ashamed also, at the divisions of Christendom. But those who have always lived within the Christian fold may be too easily dispirited by them. They are bad, but such people do not know what it looks like from without. Seen from there, what is left intact despite all the divisions, still appears (as it truly is) an immensely formidable unity. I know, for I saw it; and well our enemies know it. That unity any of us can find by going out of his own age. It is not enough, but it is more than you had thought till then. Once you are well soaked in it, if you then venture to speak, you will have an amusing experience. You will be thought a Papist when you are actually reproducing Bunyan, a Pantheist when you are quoting Aquinas, and so forth. For you have now got on to the great level viaduct which crosses the ages and which looks so high from the valleys, so low from the mountains, so narrow compared with the swamps, and so broad compared with the sheep-tracks.

The present book[2] is something of an experiment. The translation is intended for the world at large, not only for theological students. If it succeeds, other translations of other great Christian books will presumably follow. In one sense, of course, it is not the first in the field. Translations of the *Theologia Germanica*,[3] the

[1] A.E. Housman, *A Shropshire Lad* (London, 1896), stanza 40.
[2] This paper was originally published as an Introduction to St Athanasius' *The Incarnation of the Word of God*, translated by A Religious of C.S.M.V. (London, 1944).
[3] A late fourteenth-century anonymous mystical treatise.

Imitation,[1] the *Scale of Perfection*,[2] and the *Revelations* of Lady Julian of Norwich,[3] are already on the market, and are very valuable, though some of them are not very scholarly. But it will be noticed that these are all books of devotion rather than of doctrine. Now the layman or amateur needs to be instructed as well as to be exhorted. In this age his need for knowledge is particularly pressing. Nor would I admit any sharp division between the two kinds of book. For my own part, I tend to find the doctrinal books often more helpful in devotion than the devotional books, and I rather suspect that the same experience may await many others. I believe that many who find that "nothing happens" when they sit down, or kneel down, to a book of devotion, would find that the heart sings unbidden while they are working their way through a tough bit of theology with a pipe in their teeth and a pencil in their hand.

This is a good translation of a very great book. St Athanasius has suffered in popular estimation from a certain sentence in the "Athanasian Creed".[4] I will not labour the point that that work is not exactly a creed and was not by St Athanasius, for I think it is a very fine piece of writing. The words "Which Faith except every one do keep whole and undefiled, without doubt he shall perish everlastingly" are the offence. They are commonly misunderstood. The operative word is *keep*;

[1] *The Imitation of Christ*, a manual of spiritual devotion first put into circulation in 1418. The authorship has traditionally been assigned to Thomas à Kempis (*c.* 1380–1471).
[2] By Walter Hilton (d. 1396).
[3] *Sixteen Revelations of Divine Love* by Lady Julian of Norwich (*c.* 1342–after 1413).
[4] A profession of faith widely used in Western Christendom, and also known from its opening words as the *Quicunque Vult*.

not *acquire*, or even *believe*, but *keep*. The author, in fact, is not talking about unbelievers, but about deserters, not about those who have never heard of Christ, nor even those who have misunderstood and refused to accept Him, but of those who having really understood and really believed, then allow themselves, under the sway of sloth or of fashion or any other invited confusion, to be drawn away into sub-Christian modes of thought. They are a warning against the curious modern assumption that all changes of belief, however brought about, are necessarily exempt from blame.[1] But this is not my immediate concern. I mention "the creed (commonly called) of St Athanasius" only to get out of the reader's way what may have been a bogey and to put the true Athanasius in its place. His epitaph is *Athanasius contra mundum*, "Athanasius against the world". We are proud that our own country has more than once stood against the world. Athanasius did the same. He stood for the Trinitarian doctrine, "whole and undefiled", when it looked as if all the civilized world was slipping back from Christianity into the religion of Arius[2] – into one of those "sensible" synthetic religions which are so strongly recommended today and which, then as now, included among their devotees many highly cultivated clergymen. It is his glory that he did not move with the times; it is his reward that he now remains when those times, as all times do, have moved away.

When I first opened his *De Incarnatione* I soon discovered by a very simple test that I was reading a masterpiece. I knew very little Christian Greek except

[1] See Hebrews 6:4 *et seq*.
[2] Arius (*c*. 250–*c*. 336), a champion of subordinationist teaching about the Person of Christ.

that of the New Testament, and I had expected difficulties. To my astonishment I found it almost as easy as Xenophon; and only a master mind could, in the fourth century, have written so deeply on such a subject with such classical simplicity. Every page I read confirmed this impression. His approach to the Miracles is badly needed today, for it is the final answer to those who object to them as "arbitrary and meaningless violations of the laws of Nature".[1] They are here shown to be rather the re-telling in capital letters of the same message which Nature writes in her crabbed cursive hand; the very operations one would expect of Him who was so full of life that when He wished to die He had to "borrow death from others". The whole book, indeed, is a picture of the Tree of Life – a sappy and golden book, full of buoyancy and confidence. We cannot, I admit, appropriate all its confidence today. We cannot point to the high virtue of Christian living and the gay, almost mocking courage of Christian martyrdom, as a proof of our doctrines with quite that assurance which Athanasius takes as a matter of course. But whoever may be to blame for that it is not Athanasius.

---

[1] A few years after this was written, Lewis himself wrote an admirable defence, *Miracles: A Preliminary Study* (London, 1947).

4

"Horrid Red Things"
(*1944*)

Many theologians and some scientists are now ready to proclaim that the nineteenth-century "conflict between science and religion" is over and done with. But even if this is true, it is a truth known only to real theologians and real scientists – that is, to a few highly educated men. To the man in the street the conflict is still perfectly real, and in his mind it takes a form which the learned hardly dream of.

The ordinary man is not thinking of particular dogmas and particular scientific discoveries. What troubles him is an all-pervading difference of atmosphere between what he believes Christianity to be and that general picture of the universe which he has picked up from living in a scientific age. He gathers from the Creed that God has a "Son" (just as if God were a god, like Odin or Jupiter): that this Son "came down" (like a parachutist) from "Heaven", first to earth and later to some land of the dead situated beneath the earth's surface: that, still later, He ascended into the sky and took His seat in a decorated chair placed a little to the right of His Father's throne. The whole thing seems to imply a local and material heaven – a palace in the stratosphere – a flat earth and all the rest of those archaic misconceptions.

The ordinary man is well aware that we should deny all the beliefs he attributes to us and interpret our Creed in a different sense. But this by no means satisfies him. "No doubt," he thinks, "once those articles of belief are there, they can be allegorized or spiritualized away to any extent you please. But is it not plain that they would never have been there at all if the first generation of Christians had had any notion of what the real universe is like? A historian who has based his work on the misreading of a document, may afterwards (when his mistake had been exposed) exercise great ingenuity in showing that his account of a certain battle can still be reconciled with what the document records. But the point is that none of these ingenious explanations would ever have come into existence if he had read his documents correctly at the outset. They are therefore really a waste of labour; it would be manlier of him to admit his mistake and begin over again."

I think there are two things that Christians must do if they wish to convince this "ordinary" modern man. In the first place, they must make it quite clear that what will remain of the Creed after all their explanations and reinterpretations will still be something quite un-ambiguously supernatural, miraculous, and shocking. We may not believe in a flat earth and a sky-palace. But we must insist from the beginning that we believe, as firmly as any savage or theosophist, in a spirit-world which can, and does, invade the natural or phenomenal universe. For the plain man suspects that when we start explaining, we are going to explain away: that we have mythology for our ignorant hearers and are ready, when cornered by educated hearers, to reduce it to innocuous moral platitudes which no one ever dreamed of denying. And there are theologians who justify this suspicion. From them we must part company absolutely. If nothing remains except what could be equally well stated without Christian formulae, then the honest thing is to admit that Christianity is untrue and to begin over again without it.

In the second place, we must try to teach something about the difference between thinking and imagining. It is, of course, a historical error to suppose that all, or even most, early Christians believed in the sky-palace in the same sense in which we believe in the solar system. Anthropomorphism was condemned by the Church as soon as the question was explicitly before her. But some early Christians may have done this; and probably thousands never thought of their faith without anthropomorphic imagery. That is why we must distinguish the core of belief from the attendant imagining.

When I think of London I always see a picture of Euston Station. But I do not believe that London *is* Euston Station. That is a simple case, because there the thinker *knows* the imagery to be false. Now let us take a more complex one. I once heard a lady tell her daughter that if you ate too many aspirin tablets you would die. "But why?" asked the child. "If you squash them you don't find any horrid red things inside them." Obviously, when this child thought of poison she not only had an attendant image of "horrid red things", but she actually believed that poison was red. And this is an error. But how far does it invalidate her thinking about poison? She learned that an overdose of aspirin would kill you; her belief was true. She knew, within limits, which of the substances in her mother's house were poisonous. If I, staying in the house, had raised a glass of what looked like water to my lips, and the child had said, "Don't drink that. Mummie says it's poisonous," I should have been foolish to disregard the warning on the ground that "This child has an archaic and mythological idea of poison as horrid red things."

There is thus a distinction not only between thought and imagination in general, but even between thought and those images which the thinker (falsely) believes to be true. When the child learned later that poison is not always red, she would not have felt that anything essential in her beliefs about poison had been altered. She would still know, as she had always known, that poison is what kills you if you swallow it. That is the essence of poison. The erroneous beliefs about colour drop away without affecting it.

In the same way an early peasant Christian might have thought that Christ's sitting at the right hand of the Father really implied two chairs of state, in a certain spatial relation, inside a sky-palace. But if the same man afterwards received a philosophical education and discovered that God has no body, parts, or passions, and therefore neither a right hand nor a palace, he would not have felt that the essentials of his belief had been altered. What had mattered to him, even in the days of his simplicity, had not been supposed details about celestial furniture. It had been the assurance that the once crucified Master was now the supreme Agent of the unimaginable Power on whom the whole universe depends. And he would recognize that in this he had never been deceived.

The critic may still ask us why the imagery – which we admit to be untrue – should be used at all. But he has not noticed that any language we attempt to substitute for it would involve imagery that is open to all the same objections. To say that God "enters" the natural order involves just as much spatial imagery as to say that He "comes down"; one has simply substituted horizontal (or undefined) for vertical movement. To say that He is "re-absorbed" into the Noumenal is better than to say He "ascended" into Heaven, only if the picture of something dissolving in warm fluid, or being sucked into a throat, is less misleading than the picture of a bird, or a balloon, going up. All language, except about objects of sense, is metaphorical through and through. To call God a "Force" (that is, something like a wind or a dynamo) is as metaphorical as to call Him a Father or a King. On such matters we can make our language more polysyllabic and duller: we cannot make it more literal. The difficulty is not peculiar to theologians. Scientists, poets, psychoanalysts, and metaphysicians are all in the same boat:

Man's reason is in such deep insolvency to sense.[1]

Where, then, do we draw the line between explaining and "explaining away"? I do not think there is much difficulty. All that concerns the un-incarnate activities of God – His operation on that plane of being where sense cannot enter – must be taken along with imagery which we know to be, in the literal sense, untrue. But there can

[1] Robert Bridges, *The Testament of Beauty*, Book I, line 57.

be no defence for applying the same treatment to the miracles of the Incarnate God. They are recorded as events on this earth which affected human senses. They are the sort of thing we can describe literally. If Christ turned water into wine, and we had been present, we could have seen, smelled, and tasted. The story that He did so is not of the same order as His "sitting at the right hand of the Father". It is either fact, or legend, or lie. You must take it or leave it.

5

Work and Prayer

(*1945*)

"Even if I grant your point and admit that answers to prayer are theoretically possible, I shall still think they are infinitely improbable. I don't think it at all likely that God requires the ill-informed (and contradictory) advice of us humans as to how to run the world. If He is all-wise, as you say He is, doesn't He know already what is best? And if He is all-good won't He do it whether we pray or not?"

This is the case against prayer which has, in the last hundred years, intimidated thousands of people. The usual answer is that it applies only to the lowest sort of prayer, the sort that consists in asking for things to happen. The higher sort, we are told, offers no advice to God; it consists only of "communion" or intercourse with Him; and those who take this line seem to suggest that the lower kind of prayer really is an absurdity and that only children or savages would use it.

I have never been satisfied with this view. The distinction between the two sorts of prayer is a sound one; and I think on the whole (I am not quite certain) that the sort which asks for nothing is the higher or more advanced. To be in the state in which you are so at one with the will of God that you wouldn't want to alter the course of events even if you could is certainly a very high or advanced condition.

But if one simply rules out the lower kind two difficulties follow. In the first place, one has to say that the whole historical tradition of Christian prayer (including the Lord's Prayer itself) has been wrong: for it has always admitted prayers for our daily bread, for the recovery of the sick, for protection from enemies, for the conversion of the outside world and the like. In the second place, though the other kind of prayer may be "higher" if you restrict yourself to it because you have got beyond the desire to use any other, there is nothing specially "high" or "spiritual" about abstaining from prayers that make requests simply because you think they're no good. It might be a very pretty thing (but, again, I'm not absolutely certain) if a little boy never asked for cake because he was so high-minded and spiritual that he didn't want any cake. But there's nothing specially pretty about a little boy who doesn't ask because he has learned that it is no use asking. I think that the whole matter needs reconsideration.

The case against prayer (I mean the "low" or old-fashioned kind) is this. The thing you ask for is either good – for you and for the world in general – or else it is not. If it is, then a good and wise God will do it anyway. If it is not, then He won't. In neither case can your prayer make any difference. But if this argument is sound, surely it is an argument not only against praying, but against doing anything whatever?

In every action, just as in every prayer, you are trying to bring about a certain result; and this result must be good or bad. Why, then, do we not argue as the opponents of prayer argue, and say that if the intended result is good God will bring it to pass without your

41

interference, and that if it is bad He will prevent it happening whatever you do? Why wash your hands? If God intends them to be clean, they'll come clean without your washing them. If He doesn't, they'll remain dirty (as Lady Macbeth found)[1] however much soap you use. Why ask for the salt? Why put on your boots? Why do anything?

We know that we can act and that our actions produce results. Everyone who believes in God must therefore admit (quite apart from the question of prayer) that God has not chosen to write the whole of history with His own hand. Most of the events that go on in the universe are indeed out of our control, but not all. It is like a play in which the scene and the general outline of the story is fixed by the author, but certain minor details are left for the actors to improvise. It may be a mystery why He should have allowed us to cause real events at all; but it is no odder that He should allow us to cause them by praying than by any other method.

Pascal says that God "instituted prayer in order to allow His creatures the dignity of causality". It would perhaps be truer to say that He invented both prayer and physical action for that purpose. He gave us small creatures the dignity of being able to contribute to the course of events in two different ways. He made the matter of the universe such that we can (in those limits) do things to it; that is why we can wash our own hands and feed or murder our fellow creatures. Similarly, He made His own plan or plot of history such that it admits a certain amount of free play and can be modified in response to our prayers. If it is foolish and impudent to

[1] *Macbeth*, V, i, 34–57.

ask for victory in a war (on the ground that God might be expected to know best), it would be equally foolish and impudent to put on a mackintosh – does not God know best whether you ought to be wet or dry?

The two methods by which we are allowed to produce events may be called work and prayer. Both are alike in this respect – that in both we try to produce a state of affairs which God has not (or at any rate not yet) seen fit to provide "on His own". And from this point of view the old maxim *laborare est orare* (work is prayer) takes on a new meaning. What we do when we weed a field is not quite different from what we do when we pray for a good harvest. But there is an important difference all the same.

You cannot be sure of a good harvest whatever you do to a field. But you can be sure that if you pull up one weed that one weed will no longer be there. You can be sure that if you drink more than a certain amount of alcohol you will ruin your health or that if you go on for a few centuries more wasting the resources of the planet on wars and luxuries you will shorten the life of the whole human race. The kind of causality we exercise by work is, so to speak, divinely guaranteed, and therefore ruthless. By it we are free to do ourselves as much harm as we please. But the kind which we exercise by prayer is not like that; God has left Himself a discretionary power. Had He not done so, prayer would be an activity too dangerous for man and we should have the horrible state of things envisaged by Juvenal: "Enormous prayers which Heaven in anger grants."[1]

Prayers are not always – in the crude, factual sense of

[1] *Satires*, Book IV, Satire x, line 111.

the word – "granted". This is not because prayer is a weaker kind of causality, but because it is a stronger kind. When it "works" at all it works unlimited by space and time. That is why God has retained a discretionary power of granting or refusing it; except on that condition prayer would destroy us. It is not unreasonable for a headmaster to say, "Such and such things you may do according to the fixed rules of this school. But such and such other things are too dangerous to be left to general rules. If you want to do them you must come and make a request and talk over the whole matter with me in my study. And then – we'll see."

6

Two Lectures

(*1945*)

"And so," said the lecturer, "I end where I began. Evolution, development, the slow struggle upwards and onwards from crude and inchoate beginnings towards ever-increasing perfection and elaboration – that appears to be the very formula of the whole universe.

"We see it exemplified in everything we study. The oak comes from the acorn. The giant express engine of today comes from the Rocket. The highest achievements of contemporary art are in a continuous line of descent from the rude scratchings with which prehistoric man adorned the wall of his cave.

"What are the ethics and philosophy of civilized man but a miraculous elaboration of the most primitive instincts and savage taboos? Each one of us has grown, through slow pre-natal stages in which we were at first more like fish than mammals, from a particle of matter too small to be seen. Man himself springs from beasts: the organic from the inorganic. Development is the key word. The march of all things is from lower to higher."

None of this, of course, was new to me or to anyone else in the audience. But it was put very well (much better than it appears in my reproduction) and the whole voice and figure of the lecturer were impressive. At least they must have impressed me, for otherwise I cannot account for the curious dream I had that night.

I dreamed that I was still at the lecture, and the voice from the platform was still going on. But it was saying all the wrong things. At least it may have been saying the right things up to the very moment at which I began attending; but it certainly began going wrong after that. What I remembered on waking went like this: " . . . appears to be the very formula of the whole universe. We see it exemplified in everything we study. The acorn comes from a full-grown oak. The first crude engine, the Rocket, comes, not from a still cruder engine, but from something much more perfect than itself and much more complex, the mind of a man, and a man of genius. The first prehistoric drawings come, not from earlier scratchings, but from the hand and brain of human beings whose hand and brain cannot be shown to have been in any way inferior to our own; and indeed it is obvious that the man who first conceived the idea of making a picture must have been a greater genius than any of the artists who have succeeded him. The embryo with which the life of each one of us began did not originate from something even more embryonic; it originated from two fully-developed human beings, our parents. Descent, downward movement, is the key word. The march of all things is from higher to lower. The rude and imperfect thing always springs from something perfect and developed."

I did not think much of this while I was shaving, but it so happened that I had no ten o'clock pupil that morning, and when I had finished answering my letters I sat down and reflected on my dream.

It appeared to me that the Dream Lecturer had a good deal to be said for him. It is true that we do see all round us things growing up to perfection from small and rude beginnings; but then it is equally true that the small and rude beginnings themselves always come from some full-grown and developed thing. All adults were once babies, true: but then all babies were begotten and borne by adults. Corn does come from seed: but then seed comes from corn. I could even give the Dream Lecturer an example he had missed. All civilizations grow from small beginnings; but when you look into it you always find that those small beginnings themselves have been "dropped" (as an oak drops an acorn) by some other and mature civilization. The weapons and even the cookery of old Germanic barbarism are, so to speak, driftwood from the wrecked ship of Roman civilization. The starting point of Greek culture is the remains of older Minoan cultures, supplemented by oddments from civilized Egypt and Phoenicia.

But in that case, thought I, what about the first civilization of all? As soon as I asked this question I realized that the Dream Lecturer had been choosing his examples rather cautiously. He had talked only about things we can see going on around us. He had kept off the subject of absolute beginnings. He had quite correctly pointed out that in the present, and in the *historical* past, we see imperfect life coming from perfect just as much as *vice versa*. But he hadn't even attempted to answer the Real Lecturer about the beginnings of all life. The Real Lecturer's view was that when you got back far enough – back into those parts of the past which we know less about – you would find an absolute beginning, and it would be something small and imperfect.

That was a point in favour of the Real Lecturer. He at least had a theory about the absolute beginning, whereas the Dream Lecturer had slurred it over. But hadn't the Real Lecturer done a little slurring too? He had not given us a hint that his theory of the ultimate origins involved us in believing that Nature's habits have, since those days, altered completely. Her present habits show us an endless cycle – the bird coming from the egg and the egg from the bird. But he asked us to believe that the whole thing started with an egg which had been preceded by no bird. Perhaps it did. But the whole *prima facie* plausibility of his view – the ease with which the audience accepted it as something natural and obvious – depended on his slurring over the immense difference between this and the processes we actually observe. He put it over by drawing our attention to the fact that eggs develop into birds and making us forget that birds lay eggs; indeed, we have been trained to do this all our lives: trained to look at the universe with one eye shut. "Developmentalism" is made to look plausible by a kind of trick.

For the first time in my life I began to look at the question with both eyes open. In the world I know, the perfect produces the imperfect, which again becomes perfect – egg leads to bird and bird to egg – in endless succession. If there ever was a life which sprang of its own accord out of a purely inorganic universe, or a civilization which raised itself by its own shoulder-straps out of pure savagery, then this event was totally unlike the beginnings of every subsequent life and every subsequent civilization. The thing may have happened; but all its plausibility is gone. On any view, the first beginning must have been outside the ordinary processes of nature. An egg which came from no bird is no more "natural" than a bird which had existed from all eternity. And since the egg-bird-egg sequence leads us to no plausible beginning, is it not reasonable to look for the real origin somewhere outside the sequence altogether? You have to go outside the sequence of engines, into the world of men, to find the real originator of the Rocket. Is it not equally reasonable to look outside Nature for the real Originator of the natural order?

7

Meditation in a
Toolshed
(*1945*)

I was standing today in the dark toolshed. The sun was shining outside and through the crack at the top of the door there came a sunbeam. From where I stood that beam of light, with the specks of dust floating in it, was the most striking thing in the place. Everything else was almost pitch-black. I was seeing the beam, not seeing things by it.

Then I moved, so that the beam fell on my eyes. Instantly the whole previous picture vanished. I saw no toolshed, and (above all) no beam. Instead I saw, framed in the irregular cranny at the top of the door, green leaves moving on the branches of a tree outside and beyond that, ninety-odd million miles away, the sun. Looking along the beam, and looking at the beam are very different experiences.

But this is only a very simple example of the difference between looking at and looking along. A young man meets a girl. The whole world looks different when he sees her. Her voice reminds him of something he has been trying to remember all his life, and ten minutes' casual chat with her is more precious than all the favours that all other women in the world could grant. He is, as they say, "in love". Now comes a scientist and describes this young man's experience from the outside. For him it is all an affair of the young man's genes and a recognized biological stimulus. That is the difference between looking *along* the sexual impulse and looking *at* it.

When you have got into the habit of making this distinction you will find examples of it all day long. The mathematician sits thinking, and to him it seems that he is contemplating timeless and spaceless truths about quantity. But the cerebral physiologist, if he could look inside the mathematician's head, would find nothing timeless and spaceless there – only tiny movements in the grey matter. The savage dances in ecstasy at midnight before Nyonga and feels with every muscle that his dance is helping to bring the new green crops and the spring rain and the babies. The anthropologist, observing that savage, records that he is performing a fertility ritual of the type so-and-so. The girl cries over her broken doll and feels that she has lost a real friend; the psychologist says that her nascent maternal instinct has been temporarily lavished on a bit of shaped and coloured wax.

As soon as you have grasped this simple distinction, it raises a question. You get one experience of a thing when you look along it and another when you look at it. Which is the "true" or "valid" experience? Which tells you most about the thing? And you can hardly ask that question without noticing that for the last fifty years or so everyone has been taking the answer for granted. It has been assumed without discussion that if you want the true account of religion you must go, not to religious people, but to anthropologists; that if you want the true account of sexual love you must go, not to lovers, but to psychologists; that if you want to understand some "ideology" (such as medieval chivalry or the nineteenth-century idea of a "gentleman"), you must listen not to those who lived inside it, but to sociologists.

The people who look *at* things have had it all their own way; the people who look *along* things have simply been brow-beaten. It has even come to be taken for granted that the external account of a thing somehow refutes or "debunks" the account given from inside. "All these moral ideas which look so transcendental and beautiful from inside", says the wiseacre, "are really only a mass of biological instincts and inherited taboos." And no one plays the game the other way round by replying, "If you will only step inside, the things that look to you like instincts and taboos will suddenly reveal their real and transcendental nature."

That, in fact, is the whole basis of the specifically "modern" type of thought. And is it not, you will ask, a very sensible basis? For, after all, we are often deceived by things from the inside. For example, the girl who looks so wonderful while we're in love, may really be a very plain, stupid and disagreeable person. The savage's dance to Nyonga does not really cause the crops to grow. Having been so often deceived by looking along, are we not well advised to trust only to looking at? – in fact, to discount all these inside experiences?

Well, no. There are two fatal objections to discounting them *all*. And the first is this. You discount them in order to think more accurately. But you can't think at all – and therefore, of course, can't think accurately – if you have nothing to think *about*. A physiologist, for example, can study pain and find out that it "is" (whatever *is* means) such and such neural events. But the word *pain* would have no meaning for him unless he had "been inside" by actually suffering. If he had never looked *along* pain he simply wouldn't know what he was looking *at*. The very subject for his inquiries from outside exists for him only because he has, at least once, been inside.

This case is not likely to occur, because every man has felt pain. But it is perfectly easy to go on all your life giving explanations of religion, love, morality, honour and the like, without having been inside any of them. And if you do that, you are simply playing with counters. You go on explaining a thing without knowing what it is. That is why a great deal of contemporary thought is, strictly speaking, thought about nothing – all the apparatus of thought busily working in a vacuum.

The other objection is this: let us go back to the toolshed. I might have discounted what I saw when looking along the beam (i.e., the leaves moving and the sun) on the ground that it was "really only a strip of dusty light in a dark shed". That is, I might have set up as "true" my "side vision" of the beam. But then that side vision is itself an instance of the activity we call seeing. And this new instance could also be looked at from outside. I could allow a scientist to tell me that what seemed to be a beam of light in a shed was "really only an agitation of my own optic nerves". And that would be just as good (or as bad) a bit of debunking as the previous one. The picture of the beam in the toolshed would now have to be discounted just as the previous picture of the trees and the sun had been discounted. And then, where are you?

In other words, you can step outside one experience only by stepping inside another. Therefore, if all inside experiences are misleading, we are always misled. The cerebral physiologist may say, if he chooses, that the mathematician's thought is "only" tiny physical movements of the grey matter. But then what about the cerebral physiologist's own thought at that very moment? A second physiologist, looking at it, could pronounce it also to be only tiny physical movements in the first physiologist's skull. Where is the rot to end?

The answer is that we must never allow the rot to begin. We must, on pain of idiocy, deny from the very outset the idea that looking *at* is, by its own nature, intrinsically truer or better than looking *along*. One must look both *along* and *at* everything. In particular cases we shall find reason for regarding the one or the other vision as inferior. Thus the inside vision of rational thinking must be truer than the outside vision which sees only movements of the grey matter; for if the outside vision were the correct one all thought (including this thought itself) would be valueless, and this is self-contradictory. You cannot have a proof that no proofs matter. On the other hand, the inside vision of the savage's dance to Nyonga may be found deceptive because we find reason to believe that crops and babies are not really affected by it. In fact, we must take each case on its merits. But we must start with no prejudice for or against either kind of looking. We do not know in advance whether the lover or the psychologist is giving the more correct account of love, or whether both accounts are equally correct in different ways, or whether both are equally wrong. We just have to find out. But the period of brow-beating has got to end.

8

The Sermon and the Lunch
(*1945*)

"And so," said the preacher, "the home must be the foundation of our national life. It is there, all said and done, that character is formed. It is there that we appear as we really are. It is there we can fling aside the weary disguises of the outer world and be ourselves. It is there that we retreat from the noise and stress and temptation and dissipation of daily life to seek the sources of fresh strength and renewed purity..." And as he spoke I noticed that all confidence in him had departed from every member of that congregation who was under thirty. They had been listening well up to this point. Now the shufflings and coughings began. Pews creaked; muscles relaxed. The sermon, for all practical purposes, was over; the five minutes for which the preacher continued talking were a total waste of time – at least for most of us.

Whether I wasted them or not is for you to judge. I certainly did not hear any more of the sermon. I was thinking; and the starting-point of my thought was the question, "How can he? How can *he* of all people?" For I knew the preacher's own home pretty well. In fact, I had been lunching there that very day, making a fifth to the Vicar and the Vicar's wife and the son (R.A.F.) and the daughter (A.T.S.), who happened both to be on leave. I could have avoided it, but the girl had whispered to me, "For God's sake stay to lunch if they ask you. It's always a little less frightful when there's a visitor."

Lunch at the vicarage nearly always follows the same pattern. It starts with a desperate attempt on the part of the young people to keep up a bright patter of trivial conversation: trivial not because they are trivially minded (you can have real conversation with them if you get them alone), but because it would never occur to either of them to say at home anything they were really thinking, unless it is forced out of them by anger. They are talking only to try to keep their parents quiet. They fail. The Vicar, ruthlessly interrupting, cuts in on a quite different subject. He is telling us how to re-educate Germany. He has never been there and seems to know nothing either of German history or the German language. "But Father," begins the son, and gets no further. His mother is now talking, though nobody knows exactly when she began. She is in the middle of a complicated story about how badly some neighbour has treated her. Though it goes on a long time, we never learn either how it began or how it ended: it is all middle. "Mother, that's not quite fair," says the daughter at last. "Mrs Walker never said–" but her father's voice booms in again. He is telling his son about the organization of the R.A.F. So it goes on until either the Vicar or his wife says something so preposterous that the boy or the girl contradicts and insists on making the contradiction heard. The real minds of the young people have at last been called into action. They talk fiercely, quickly, contemptuously. They have facts and logic on their side. There is an answering flare up from the parents. The father storms; the mother is (oh, blessed domestic queen's move!) "hurt" – plays pathos for all she is worth. The daughter becomes ironical. The father and son, elaborately ignoring each other, start talking to me. The lunch party is in ruins.

The memory of that lunch worries me during the last few minutes of the sermon. I am not worried by the fact that the Vicar's practice differs from his precept. That is, no doubt, regrettable, but it is nothing to the purpose. As Dr Johnson said, precept may be very sincere (and, let us add, very profitable) where practice is very imperfect,[1] and no one but a fool would discount a doctor's warnings about alcoholic poisoning because the doctor himself drank too much. What worries me is the fact that the Vicar is not telling us at all that home life is difficult and has, like every form of life, its own proper temptations and corruptions. He keeps on talking as if "home" were a panacea, a magical charm which of itself was bound to produce happiness and virtue. The trouble is not that he is insincere but that he is a fool. He is not talking from his own experience of family life at all: he is automatically reproducing a sentimental tradition – and it happens to be a false tradition. That is why the congregation have stopped listening to him.

If Christian teachers wish to recall Christian people to domesticity – and I, for one, believe that people must be recalled to it – the first necessity is to stop telling lies about home life and to substitute realistic teaching. Perhaps the fundamental principles would be something like this.

[1] James Boswell, *Life of Johnson*, ed. George Birkbeck Hill (Oxford, 1934), Vol. IV, p. 397 (2nd December 1784).

First and Second Things

1. Since the Fall no organization or way of life whatever has a natural tendency to go right. In the Middle Ages some people thought that if only they entered a religious order they would find themselves automatically becoming holy and happy: the whole native literature of the period echoes with the exposure of that fatal error. In the nineteenth century some people thought that monogamous family life would automatically make them holy and happy; the savage anti-domestic literature of modern times – the Samuel Butlers, the Gosses, the Shaws – delivered the answer. In both cases the "debunkers" may have been wrong about principles and may have forgotten the maxim *abusus non tollit usum*:[1] but in both cases they were pretty right about matters of fact. Both family life and monastic life were often detestable, and it should be noticed that the serious defenders of both are well aware of the dangers and free of the sentimental illusion. The author of the *Imitation of Christ* knows (no one better) how easily monastic life goes wrong. Charlotte M. Yonge makes it abundantly clear that domesticity is no passport to heaven on earth but an arduous vocation – a sea full of hidden rocks and perilous ice shores only to be navigated by one who uses a celestial chart. That is the first point on which we must be absolutely clear. The family, like the nation, can be offered to God, can be converted and redeemed, and will then become the channel of particular blessings and graces. But, like everything else that is human, it needs redemption. Unredeemed, it will produce only particular temptations, corruptions, and miseries. Charity begins at home: so does uncharity.

[1] The abuse does not abolish the use.

2. By the conversion or sanctification of family life we must be careful to mean something more than the preservation of "love" in the sense of natural affection. Love (in that sense) is not enough. Affection, as distinct from charity, is not a cause of lasting happiness. Left to its natural bent affection becomes in the end greedy, naggingly solicitous, jealously exacting, timorous. It suffers agony when its object is absent – but is not repaid by any long enjoyment when the object is present. Even at the Vicar's lunch table affection was partly the cause of the quarrel. That son would have borne patiently and humorously from any other old man the silliness which enraged him in his father. It is because he still (in some fashion) "cares" that he is impatient. The Vicar's wife would not be quite that endless whimper of self-pity which she now is if she did not (in a sense) "love" the family: the continued disappointment of her continued and ruthless demand for sympathy, for affection, for appreciation has helped to make her what she is. I do not think this aspect of affection is nearly enough noticed by most popular moralists. The greed to be loved is a fearful thing. Some of those who say (and almost with pride) that they live only for love come, at last, to live in incessant resentment.

3. We must realize the yawning pitfall in that very characteristic of home life which is so often glibly paraded as its principal attraction. "It is there that we appear as we really are: it is there that we can fling aside the disguises and be ourselves." These words, in the Vicar's mouth, were only too true and he showed at the lunch table what they meant. Outside his own house he behaves with ordinary courtesy. He would not have inter-

rupted any other young man as he interrupted his son. He would not, in any other society, have talked confident nonsense about subjects of which he was totally ignorant: or, if he had, he would have accepted correction with good temper. In fact, he values home as the place where he can "be himself" in the sense of trampling on all the restraints which civilized humanity has found indispensable for tolerable social intercourse. And this, I think, is very common. What chiefly distinguishes domestic from public conversation is surely very often simply its selfishness, slovenliness, incivility – even brutality. And it will often happen that those who praise home life most loudly are the worst offenders in this respect: they praise it – they are always glad to get home, hate the outer world, can't stand visitors, can't be bothered meeting people, etc. – because the freedoms in which they indulge themselves at home have ended by making them unfit for civilized society. If they practised elsewhere the only behaviour they now find "natural" they would simply be knocked down.

4. How, then, *are* people to behave at home? If a man can't be comfortable and unguarded, can't take his ease and "be himself" in his own house, where can he? That is, I confess, the trouble. The answer is an alarming one. There is *nowhere* this side of heaven where one can safely lay the reins on the horse's neck. It will never be lawful simply to "be ourselves" until "ourselves" have become sons of God. It is all there in the hymn – "Christian, seek not yet repose." This does not mean, of course, that there is no difference between home life and general society. It does mean that home life has its own rule of courtesy – a code more intimate, more

subtle, more sensitive, and, therefore, in some ways more difficult, than that of the outer world.

5. Finally, must we not teach that if the home is to be a means of grace it must be a place of *rules*? There cannot be a common life without a *regula*. The alternative to rule is not freedom but the unconstitutional (and often unconscious) tyranny of the most selfish member.

In a word, must we not either cease to preach domesticity or else begin to preach it seriously? Must we not abandon sentimental eulogies and begin to give practical advice on the high, hard, lovely, and adventurous art of really creating the Christian family?

9

On the Transmission
of Christianity
(*1946*)

During the war we turn with quickened interest from the newspaper accounts of the fighting to the report of any man who has just returned from taking part in it himself. The manuscript of this little book[1] when it was first put into my hands gave me a similar excitement. Discussions on education and on religious education are admirable things; but here we have something different – a first-hand record of the results which the existing system is actually producing while we discuss. Its value is enhanced by the fact that the author is not a minister of education, nor a headmaster, nor a clergyman, nor even a professional teacher. The facts he records are facts against which he ran his head unexpectedly, almost (you might say) accidentally, while doing a particular war-time job.

There are, of course, other things beside this in the book. But I emphasize its purely documentary value because that seems to me to be far the most important

[1] This paper was originally published as a Preface to G.B. Sandhurst's book, *How Heathen is Britain?* (London, 1946), in which Mr Sandhurst describes his work with a class of young men in an attempt to discover what their views were about Man and the Godhead of Christ.

thing about it – the thing on which public attention ought to be focused. The abstracts of the author's lectures – or rather openings of discussions – are indeed full of interest, and many will wish to comment on them. They are the part of the book which it is easiest to discuss. But I insist that to concentrate on that part is an evasion.

When every allowance has been made for the possibility (delightfully unsuspected by himself) that the author has unusual talents as a teacher, two facts still emerge from his record unshaken. Firstly, that the content of, and the case for, Christianity, are not put before most schoolboys under the present system; and secondly, that when they are so put a majority find them acceptable. The importance of these two facts is that between them they blow away a whole fog of "reasons for the decline of religion" which are often advanced and often believed. If we had noticed that the young men of the present day found it harder and harder to get the right answers to sums, we should consider that this had been adequately explained the moment we discovered that schools had for some years ceased to teach arithmetic. After that discovery we should turn a deaf ear to people who offered explanations of a vaguer and larger kind – people who said that the influence of Einstein had sapped the ancestral belief in fixed numerical relations, or that gangster films had undermined the desire to get right answers, or that the evolution of consciousness was now entering on its post–arithmetical phase. Where a clear and simple explanation completely covers the facts no other explanation is in court. If the younger generation have never been told what the Christians say and never heard any arguments in defence of it, then their agnosticism or indifference is fully explained. There is no need to look any further: no need to talk about the general intellectual climate of the age, the influence of mechanistic civilization on the character of urban life. And having discovered that the cause of their ignorance is lack of instruction, we have also discovered the remedy. There is nothing in the nature of the younger generation which incapacitates them for receiving Christianity. If any one is prepared to tell them, they are apparently ready to hear.

I allow, of course, that the explanation which our author has discovered merely puts the problem a generation further back. The young people today are un-Christian because their teachers have been either unwilling or unable to transmit Christianity to them. For the impotence or unbelief of their teachers, larger and, no doubt, vaguer explanations are to be sought. But that, be it noted, is a historical problem. The schoolmasters of today are, for the most part, the undergraduates of twenty years ago – the products of the "post-war" period. It is the mental climate of the Twenties that now dominates the from room class. In other words, the sources of unbelief among young people today do not lie in those young people. The outlook which they have – until they are taught better – is a backwash from an earlier period. It is nothing intrinsic to themselves which holds them back from the Faith.

This very obvious fact – that each generation is taught by an earlier generation – must be kept very firmly in mind. The beliefs which boys fresh from school now hold are largely the beliefs of the Twenties. The beliefs which boys from school will hold in the Sixties will be largely those of the undergraduates of today. The moment we forget this we begin to talk nonsense about education. We talk of the views of contemporary adolescence as if some peculiarity in contemporary adolescence had produced them out of itself. In reality, they are usually a delayed result – for the mental world also has its time-bombs – of obsolete adolescence, now middle-aged and dominating its form room. Hence the futility of many schemes for education. None can give to another what he does not possess himself. No generation can bequeath to its successor what it has not got. You may frame the syllabus as you please. But when you have planned and reported *ad nauseam*, if we are sceptical we shall teach only scepticism to our pupils, if fools only folly, if vulgar only vulgarity, if saints sanctity, if heroes heroism. Education is only the most fully conscious of the channels whereby each generation influences the next. It is not a closed system. Nothing which was not in the teachers can flow from them into the pupils. We shall all admit that a man who knows no Greek himself cannot teach Greek to his form: but it is equally certain that a man whose mind was formed in a period of cynicism and disillusion, cannot teach hope or fortitude.

A society which is predominantly Christian will propagate Christianity through its schools: one which is not, will not. All the ministries of education in the world cannot alter this law. We have, in the long run, little either to hope or fear from government.

The State may take education more and more firmly under its wing. I do not doubt that by so doing it can foster conformity, perhaps even servility, up to a point; the power of the State to deliberalize a profession is undoubtedly very great. But all the teaching must still be done by concrete human individuals. The State has to use the men who exist. Nay, as long as we remain a democracy, it is men who give the State its powers. And over these men, until all freedom is extinguished, the free winds of opinion blow. Their minds are formed by influences which government cannot control. And as they come to be, so will they teach. Let the abstract scheme of education be what it will: its actual operation will be what the men make it. No doubt, there will be in each generation of teachers a percentage, perhaps even a majority, of government tools. But I do not think it is they who will determine the actual character of the education. The boy – and perhaps especially the English boy – has a sound instinct. The teaching of one true man will carry further and print deeper than that of a dozen white Babus. A minister of education (going back, unless I am mistaken, as far as Julian the Apostate[1] for his precedent) may banish Christian clergy from the schools. But if the wind of opinion is blowing in the Christian direction, it will make no difference. It may even do us good; and the minister will have been unknowingly "the goddes boteler".[2]

We are often told that education is a key position. That is very false in one sense and very true in another. If it means that you can do any great thing by interfering with existing schools, altering curricula and the like, it is very false. As the teachers are, so they will teach. Your

[1] Roman emperor A.D. 361–3.
[2] Chaucer, *The Hous of Fame*, Book II, line 592.

"reform" may incommode and overwork them, but it will not radically alter the total effect of their teaching. Planning has no magic whereby it can elicit figs from thistles or choke-pears from vines. The rich, sappy, fruit-laden tree will bear sweetness and strength and spiritual health: the dry, prickly, withered tree will teach hate, jealousy, suspicion, and inferiority complex – whatever you *tell* it to teach. They will do it unknowingly and all day long. But if we mean that to make adult Christians now and even beyond that circle, to spread the immediately sub-Christian perceptions and virtues, the rich Platonic or Virgilian *penumbra* of the Faith, and thus to alter the type who will be teachers in the future – if we mean that to do this is to perform the greatest of all services for our descendants, then it is very true.

So at least it seems to me: I do not know how far the author would agree with me. He has exposed the actual workings of modern education. To blame the schoolmasters of the last ten years for it would be ridiculous. The majority of them failed to hand on Christianity because they had it not: will you blame a eunuch because he gets no children or a stone because it yields no blood? The minority, isolated in a hostile environment, have probably done all they could, have perhaps done wonders: but little was in their power. Our author has also shown that the ignorance and incredulity of the pupils are very often removable – their roots far shallower than we had feared. I do not draw from this moral that it is now our business to "get our teeth into the schools". For one thing, I do not think we shall be allowed to. It is unlikely that in the next forty years England will have a government which would encourage or even tolerate any radically Christian elements in its State system of education. Where the tide flows towards increasing State control, Christianity, with its claims in one way personal and in the other way ecumenical and both ways antithetical to omnicompetent government, must always in fact (though not for a long time yet in words) be treated as an enemy. Like learning, like the family, like any ancient and liberal profession, like the common law, it gives the individual a standing ground against the State. Hence Rousseau, the father of the totalitarians, said wisely enough, from his own point of view, of Christianity, *Je ne connais rien de plus contraire à l'esprit social*.[1] In the second place, even if we were permitted to force a Christian curriculum on the existing schools with the existing teachers we should only be making masters hypocrites and hardening thereby the pupils' hearts.

I am speaking, of course, of large schools on which a secular character is already stamped. If any man, in some little corner out of the reach of the omnicompetent, can make, or preserve a really Christian school, that is another matter. His duty is plain.

I do not, therefore, think that our hope of re-baptizing England lies in trying to "get at" the schools. Education is not *in that sense* a key position. To convert one's adult neighbour and one's adolescent neighbour (just free from school) is the practical thing. The cadet, the undergraduate, the young worker in the C.W.U. are obvious targets: but any one and every one is a target. If you make the adults of today Christian, the children of tomorrow will receive a Christian education.

[1] I know nothing more opposed to the social spirit.

What a society has, that, be sure, and nothing else, it will hand on to its young. The work is urgent, for men perish around us. But there is no need to be uneasy about the ultimate event. As long as Christians have children and non-Christians do not, one need have no anxiety for the next century. Those who worship the Life-Force do not do much about transmitting it: those whose hopes are all based on the terrestrial future do not entrust much to it. If these processes continue, the final issue can hardly be in doubt.

10

The Decline of Religion
(*1946*)

From what I see of junior Oxford at present it would be quite easy to draw opposite conclusions about the religious predicament of what we call "the rising generation", though in reality the undergraduate body includes men and women almost as much divided from one another in age, outlook and experience as they are divided from the dons. Plenty of evidence can be produced to show that religion is in its last decline among them, or that a revival of interest in religion is one of their most noticeable characteristics. And in fact something that may be called "a decline" and something that may be called "a revival" are both going on. It will be perhaps more useful to attempt to understand both than to try our luck at "spotting the winner".

The "decline of religion" so often lamented (or welcomed) is held to be shown by empty chapels. Now it is quite true that chapels which were full in 1900 are empty in 1946. But this change was not gradual. It occurred at the precise moment when chapel ceased to be compulsory. It was not in fact a decline; it was a precipice. The sixty men who had come because chapel was a little later than "rollers"[1] (its only alternative)

[1] After there came to be a number of non-Anglican students in the Oxford colleges, those students who did not wish to attend the

70

came no more; the five Christians remained. The withdrawal of compulsion did not create a new religious situation, but only revealed the situation which had long existed. And this is typical of the "decline in religion" all over England.

In every class and every part of the country the visible practice of Christianity has grown very much less in the last fifty years. This is often taken to show that the nation as a whole has passed from a Christian to a secular outlook. But if we judge the nineteenth century from the books it wrote, the outlook of our grandfathers (with a very few exceptions) was quite as secular as our own. The novels of Meredith, Trollope and Thackeray are not written either by or for men who see this world as the vestibule of eternity, who regard pride as the greatest of the sins, who desire to be poor in spirit, and look for a supernatural salvation. Even more significant is the absence from Dickens' *Christmas Carol* of any interest in the Incarnation. Mary, the Magi, and the Angels are replaced by "spirits" of his own invention, and the animals present are not the ox and ass in the stable but the goose and turkey in the poulterer's shop. Most striking of all is the thirty-third chapter of *The Antiquary*, where Lord Glenallan forgives old Elspeth for her intolerable wrong. Glenallan has been painted by Scott as a life-long penitent and ascetic, a man whose every thought has been for years fixed on the super-

---

morning chapel service were required to report to the Dean five or ten minutes before the service and have their names put on his roll-call. Thus the "rollers" who did not go to chapel had to be up before those who did go. Neither chapel service nor the Dean's roll-call is compulsory now.

natural. But when he has to forgive, no motive of a Christian kind is brought into play: the battle is won by "the generosity of his nature". It does not occur to Scott that his fasts, his solitudes, his beads and his confessor, however useful as romantic "properties", could be effectively connected with a serious action which concerns the plot of the book.

I am anxious here not to be misunderstood. I do not mean that Scott was not a brave, generous, honourable man and a glorious writer. I mean that in his work, as in that of most of his contemporaries, only secular and natural values are taken seriously. Plato and Virgil are, in that sense, nearer to Christianity than they.

Thus the "decline of religion" becomes a very ambiguous phenomenon. One way of putting the truth would be that the religion which has declined was not Christianity. It was a vague Theism with a strong and virile ethical code, which, far from standing over against the "World", was absorbed into the whole fabric of English institutions and sentiment and therefore demanded churchgoing as (at best) a part of loyalty and good manners or (at worst) a proof of respectability. Hence a social pressure, like the withdrawal of the compulsion, did not create a new situation. The new freedom first allowed accurate observations to be made. When no man goes to church except because he seeks Christ the number of actual believers can at last be discovered. It should be added that this new freedom was partly caused by the very conditions which it revealed. If the various anti-clerical and anti-theistic forces at work in the nineteenth century had had to attack a solid phalanx of radical Christians the story might have been different. But mere "religion" – "morality tinged with emotion", "what a man does with his solitude", "the religion of all good men" – has little power of resistance. It is not good at saying No.

The decline of "religion", thus understood, seems to me in some ways a blessing. At the very worst it makes the issue clear. To the modern undergraduate Christianity is, at least, one of the intellectual options. It is, so to speak, on the agenda: it can be discussed, and a conversion may follow. I can remember times when this was much more difficult. "Religion" (as distinct from Christianity) was too vague to be discussed ("too sacred to be lightly mentioned") and so mixed up with sentiment and good form as to be one of the embarrassing subjects. If it had to be spoken of, it was spoken of in a hushed, medical voice. Something of the shame of the Cross is, and ought to be, irremovable. But the merely social and sentimental embarrassment is gone. The fog of "religion" has lifted; the positions and numbers of both armies can be observed; and real shooting is now possible.

The decline of "religion" is no doubt a bad thing for the "World". By it all the things that made England a fairly happy country are, I suppose, endangered: the comparative purity of her public life, the comparative humanity of her police, and the possibility of some mutual respect and kindness between political opponents. But I am not clear that it makes conversions to Christianity rarer or more difficult: rather the reverse. It makes the choice more unescapable. When the Round Table is broken every man must follow either Galahad or Mordred: middle things are gone.

So much for the Decline of Religion; now for a Christian Revival. Those who claim that there is such a Revival would point to the success (I mean success in the sense that it can be tested by sales) of several explicitly and even violently Christian writers, the apparent popularity of lectures on theological subjects, and the brisk atmosphere of not unfriendly discussion on them in which we live. They point, in fact, to what I have heard described as "the high-brow Christian racket". It is difficult to describe the phenomenon in quite neutral terms: but perhaps no one would deny that Christianity is now "on the map" among the younger *intelligentsia* as it was not, say, in 1920. Only freshmen now talk as if the anti-Christian position were self-evident. The days of "simple un-faith" are as dead as those of "simple faith".

At this those who are on the same side as myself are quite properly pleased. We have cause to give thanks: and the comments which I have to add proceed, I hope, not from a natural middle-aged desire to pour cold water into any soup within reach, but only from a desire to forestall, and therefore to disarm, possible disappointments.

In the first place, it must be admitted by anyone who accepts Christianity, that an increased interest in it, or even a growing measure of intellectual assent to it, is a very different thing from the conversion of England or even of a single soul. Conversion requires an alteration of the will, and an alteration which, in the last resort, does not occur without the intervention of the supernatural. I do not in the least agree with those who therefore conclude that the spread of an intellectual (and imaginative) climate favourable to Christianity is useless. You do not prove munition workers useless by showing that they cannot themselves win battles, however proper this reminder would be if they attempted to claim the honour due to fighting men. If the intellectual climate is such that, when a man comes to the crisis at which he must either accept or reject Christ, his reason and imagination are not on the wrong side, then his conflict will be fought out under favourable conditions. Those who help to produce and spread such a climate are therefore doing useful work: and yet no such great matter after all. Their share is a modest one; and it is always possible that nothing – nothing whatever – may come of it. Far higher than they stands that character whom, to the best of my knowledge, the present Christian movement has not yet produced – the *Preacher* in the full sense, the Evangelist, the man on fire, the man who infects. The propagandist, the apologist, only represents John Baptist: the Preacher represents the Lord Himself. He will be sent – or else he will not. But unless he comes we mere Christian intellectuals will not effect very much. That does not mean we should down tools.

In the second place we must remember that a widespread and lively interest in a subject is precisely what we call a Fashion. And it is the nature of Fashions not to last. The present Christian movement may, or may not, have a long run ahead of it. But sooner or later it must lose the public ear; in a place like Oxford such changes are extraordinarily rapid. Bradley and the other idealists fell in a few terms, the Douglas scheme even more suddenly, the Vorticists overnight.[1] (Who now re-

[1] F.H. Bradley (1846–1924) was a Fellow of Merton College, Oxford, and the author of *Appearance and Reality* (London, 1893). Major C.H. Douglas, a socio-economist, wrote, among other works, *Social Credit* (London, 1933). The Vorticists were a school of artists of the 1920s.

members Pogo?[1] Who now reads *Childermass?*[2]) Whatever in our present success mere fashion has given us, mere fashion will presently withdraw. The real conversions will remain: but nothing else will. In that sense we may be on the brink of a real and permanent Christian revival: but it will work slowly and obscurely and in small groups. The present sunshine (if I may so call it) is certainly temporary. The grain must be got into the barns before the wet weather comes.

This mutability is the fate of all movements, fashions, intellectual climates and the like. But a Christian movement is also up against something sterner than the mere fickleness of taste. We have not yet had (at least in junior Oxford) any really bitter opposition. But if we have many more successes, this will certainly appear. The enemy has not yet thought it worth while to fling his whole weight against us. But he soon will. This happens in the history of every Christian movement, beginning with the Ministry of Christ Himself. At first it is welcome to all who have no special reason for opposing it: at this stage he who is not against it is for it. What men notice is its difference from those aspects of the World which they already dislike. But later on, as the real meaning of the Christian claim becomes apparent, its demand for total surrender, the sheer chasm between Nature and Supernature, men are increasingly "offended". Dislike, terror, and finally hatred succeed: none who will not give it what it asks (and it asks all) can endure it: all who are not with it are against it. That is

---

[1] No one, practically. As far as I can discover, Pogo, or the Pogo-stick, which was invented in 1922, is a stilt with a spring on which the player jumps about.

[2] *Childermass* is by P. Wyndham Lewis (London, 1928).

why we must cherish no picture of the present intellectual movement simply growing and spreading and finally reclaiming millions by sweet reasonableness. Long before it became as important as that the real opposition would have begun, and to be on the Christian side would be costing a man (at the least) his career. But remember, in England the opposition will quite likely be *called* Christianity (or Christo-democracy, or British Christianity, or something of that kind).

I think – but how should I know? – that all is going reasonably well. But it is early days. Neither our armour nor our enemies' is yet engaged. Combatants always tend to imagine that the war is further on than it really is.

11

Vivisection
(*1947*)

It is the rarest thing in the world to hear a rational discussion of vivisection. Those who disapprove of it are commonly accused of "sentimentality", and very often their arguments justify the accusation. They paint pictures of pretty little dogs on dissecting tables. But the other side lie open to exactly the same charge. They also often defend the practice by drawing pictures of suffering women and children whose pain can be relieved (we are assured) only by the fruits of vivisection. The one appeal, quite as clearly as the other, is addressed to emotion, to the particular emotion we call pity. And neither appeal proves anything. If the thing is right – and if right at all, it is a duty – then pity for the animal is one of the temptations we must resist in order to perform that duty. If the thing is wrong, then pity for human suffering is precisely the temptation which will most probably lure us into doing that wrong thing. But the real question – *whether* it is right or wrong – remains meanwhile just where it was.

A rational discussion of this subject begins by inquiring whether pain is, or is not, an evil. If it is not, then the case against vivisection falls. But then so does the case for vivisection. If it is not defended on the ground that it reduces human suffering, on what ground can it be defended? And if pain is not an evil, why should human suffering be reduced? We must therefore assume as a basis for the whole discussion that pain is an evil, otherwise there is nothing to be discussed.

Now if pain is an evil then the infliction of pain, considered in itself, must clearly be an evil act. But there are such things as necessary evils. Some acts which would be bad, simply in themselves, may be excusable and even laudable when they are necessary means to a greater good. In saying that the infliction of pain, simply in itself, is bad, we are not saying that pain ought never to be inflicted. Most of us think that it can rightly be inflicted for a good purpose – as in dentistry or just and reformatory punishment. The point is that it always requires justification. On the man whom we find inflicting pain rests the burden of showing why an act which in itself would be simply bad is, in those particular circumstances, good. If we find a man giving pleasure it is for us to prove (if we criticize him) that his action is wrong. But if we find a man inflicting pain it is for him to prove that his action is right. If he cannot, he is a wicked man.

Now vivisection can only be defended by showing it to be right that one species should suffer in order that another species should be happier. And here we come to the parting of the ways. The Christian defender and the ordinary "scientific" (i.e., naturalistic) defender of vivisection, have to take quite different lines.

The Christian defender, especially in the Latin countries, is very apt to say that we are entitled to do anything we please to animals because they "have no souls". But what does this mean? If it means that

79

animals have no consciousness, then how is this known? They certainly behave as if they had, or at least the higher animals do. I myself am inclined to think that far fewer animals than is supposed have what we should recognize as consciousness. But that is only an opinion. Unless we know on other grounds that vivisection is right we must not take the moral risk of tormenting them on a mere opinion. On the other hand, the statement that they "have no souls" may mean that they have no moral responsibilities and are not immortal. But the absence of "soul" in that sense makes the infliction of pain upon them not easier but harder to justify. For it means that animals cannot deserve pain, nor profit morally by the discipline of pain, nor be recompensed by happiness in another life for suffering in this. Thus all the factors which render pain more tolerable or make it less totally evil in the case of human beings will be lacking in the beasts. "Soullessness", in so far as it is relevant to the question at all, is an argument against vivisection.

The only rational line for the Christian vivisectionist to take is to say that the superiority of man over beast is a real objective fact, guaranteed by Revelation, and that the propriety of sacrificing beast to man is a logical consequence. We are "worth more than many sparrows",[1] and in saying this we are not merely expressing a natural preference for our own species simply because it is our own but conforming to a hierarchical order created by God and really present in the universe whether any one acknowledges it or not. The position may not be satisfactory. We may fail to see how a

[1] Matthew 10:31.

80

benevolent Deity could wish us to draw such conclusions from the hierarchical order He has created. We may find it difficult to formulate a human right of tormenting beasts in terms which would not equally imply an angelic right of tormenting men. And we may feel that though objective superiority is rightly claimed for men, yet that very superiority ought partly to *consist in* not behaving like a vivisector: that we ought to prove ourselves better than the beasts precisely by the fact of acknowledging duties to them which they do not acknowledge to us. But on all these questions different opinions can be honestly held. If on grounds of our real, divinely ordained, superiority a Christian pathologist thinks it right to vivisect, and does so with scrupulous care to avoid the least dram or scruple of unnecessary pain, in a trembling awe at the responsibility which he assumes, and with a vivid sense of the high mode in which human life must be lived if it is to justify the sacrifices made for it, then (whether we agree with him or not) we can respect his point of view.

But of course the vast majority of vivisectors have no such theological background. They are most of them naturalistic and Darwinian. Now here, surely, we come up against a very alarming fact. The very same people who will most contemptuously brush aside any consideration of animal suffering if it stands in the way of "research" will also, on another context, most vehemently deny that there is any radical difference between man and the other animals. On the naturalistic view the beasts are at bottom just the same *sort* of thing as ourselves. Man is simply the cleverest of the anthropoids. All the grounds on which a Christian might defend vivisection are thus cut from under our feet. We sacrifice other species to our own not because our own has any objective metaphysical privilege over others, but simply because it is ours. It may be very natural to have this loyalty to our own species, but let us hear no more from the naturalists about the "sentimentality" of anti-vivisectionists. If loyalty to our own species, preference for man simply because we are men, is not a sentiment, then what is? It may be a good sentiment or a bad one. But a sentiment it certainly is. Try to base it on logic and see what happens!

But the most sinister thing about modern vivisection is this. If a mere sentiment justifies cruelty, why stop at a sentiment for the whole human race? There is also a sentiment for the white man against the black, for a *Herrenvolk* against the non-Aryans, for "civilized" or "progressive" peoples against "savages" or "backward" peoples. Finally, for our own country, party or class against others. Once the old Christian idea of a total difference in kind between man and beast has been abandoned, then no argument for experiments on animals can be found which is not also an argument for experiments on inferior men. If we cut up beasts simply because they cannot prevent us and because we are backing our own side in the struggle for existence, it is only logical to cut up imbeciles, criminals, enemies or capitalists for the same reasons. Indeed, experiments on men have already begun. We all hear that Nazi scientists have done them. We all suspect that our own scientists may begin to do so, in secret, at any moment.

The alarming thing is that the vivisectors have won the first round. In the nineteenth and eighteenth centuries a man was not stamped as a "crank" for protesting against vivisection. Lewis Carroll protested, if I remember his famous letter correctly, on the very same ground which I have just used.[1] Dr Johnson – a man whose mind had as much *iron* in it as any man's – protested in a note on *Cymbeline* which is worth quoting in full. In Act I, scene v, the Queen explains to the Doctor that she wants poisons to experiment on "such creatures as We count not worth the hanging – but none human".[2] The Doctor replies:

> Your Highness
> Shall from this practice but make hard your heart.[3]

Johnson comments: "The thought would probably have been more amplified, had our author lived to be shocked with such experiments as have been published in later times, by a race of men that have practised tortures without pity, and related them without shame, and are yet suffered to erect their heads among human beings."[4]

The words are his, not mine, and in truth we hardly dare in these days to use such calmly stern language. The reason why we do not dare is that the other side has in fact won. And though cruelty even to beasts is an important matter, their victory is symptomatic of matters more important still. The victory of vivisection marks a

---

[1] "Vivisection as a Sign of the Times", *The Works of Lewis Carroll*, ed. Roger Lancelyn Green (London, 1965), pp. 1089–92. See also "Some Popular Fallacies about Vivisection", ibid., pp. 1092–1100.

[2] Shakespeare, *Cymbeline*, I, v, 19–20.

[3] ibid., 23.

[4] *Johnson on Shakespeare: Essays and Notes Selected and Set Forth with an Introduction by Sir Walter Raleigh (London, 1908), p. 181.*

great advance in the triumph of ruthless, non-moral utilitarianism over the old world of ethical law; a triumph in which we, as well as animals, are already the victims, and of which Dachau and Hiroshima mark the more recent achievements. In justifying cruelty to animals we put ourselves also on the animal level. We choose the jungle and must abide by our choice.

You will notice I have spent no time in discussing what actually goes on in the laboratories. We shall be told, of course, that there is surprisingly little cruelty. That is a question with which, at present, I have nothing to do. We must first decide what should be allowed: after that it is for the police to discover what is already being done.

12

Modern Translations
of the Bible
(1947)

It is possible that the reader who opens this volume[1] on
the counter of a bookshop may ask himself why we need a
new translation of any part of the Bible, and, if of any, why
of the Epistles. "Do we not already possess", it may be
said, "in the Authorized Version the most beautiful
rendering which any language can boast?" Some people
whom I have met go even further and feel that a modern
translation is not only unnecessary but even offensive.
They cannot bear to see the time-honoured words
altered; it seems to them irreverent.

There are several answers to such people. In the first
place the kind of objection which they feel to a new
translation is very like the objection which was once felt to
any English translation at all. Dozens of sincerely pious
people in the sixteenth century shuddered at the idea of
turning the time-honoured Latin of the Vulgate into our
common and (as they thought) "barbarous" English. A
sacred truth seemed to them to have lost its sanctity when
it was stripped of the polysyllabic Latin, long heard at

[1] This essay was originally published as an Introduction to J.B.
Phillips' *Letters to Young Churches: A Translation of the New
Testament Epistles* (London, 1947).

Mass and at Hours, and put into "language such as men do use" – language steeped in all the commonplace associations of the nursery, the inn, the stable and the street. The answer then was the same as the answer now. The only kind of sanctity which Scripture can lose (or at least New Testament Scripture) by being modernized is an accidental kind which it never had for its writers or its earliest readers. The New Testament in the original Greek is not a work of literary art: it is not written in a solemn, ecclesiastical language, it is written in the sort of Greek which was spoken over the Eastern Mediterranean after Greek had become an international language and therefore lost its real beauty and subtlety. In it we see Greek used by people who have no real feeling for Greek words because Greek words are not the words they spoke when they were children. It is a sort of "basic" Greek; a language without roots in the soil, a utilitarian, commercial and administrative language. Does this shock us? It ought not to, except as the Incarnation itself ought to shock us. The same divine humility which decreed that God should become a baby at a peasant-woman's breast, and later an arrested field-preacher in the hands of the Roman police, decreed also that He should be preached in a vulgar, prosaic and unliterary language. If you can stomach the one, you can stomach the other. The Incarnation is in that sense an irreverent doctrine: Christianity, in that sense, an incurably irreverent religion. When we expect that it should have come before the World in all the beauty that we now feel in the Authorized Version we are as wide of the mark as the Jews were in expecting that the Messiah would come as a great earthly King. The real sanctity, the real beauty and sublimity of the New Testament (as of Christ's life) are of a different sort: miles deeper or *further in*.

In the second place, the Authorized Version has ceased to be a good (that is, a clear) translation. It is no longer modern English: the meanings of words have changed. The same antique glamour which has made it (in the superficial sense) so "beautiful", so "sacred", so "comforting", and so "inspiring", has also made it in many places unintelligible. Thus where St Paul says "I know nothing against myself", it translates "I know nothing by myself".[1] That was a good translation (though even then rather old-fashioned) in the sixteenth century: to the modern reader it means either nothing, or something quite different from what St Paul said. The truth is that if we are to have translation at all we must have periodical re-translation. There is no such thing as translating a book into another language once and for all, for a language is a changing thing. If your son is to have clothes it is no good buying him a suit once and for all: he will grow out of it and have to be re-clothed.

And finally, though it may seem a sour paradox – we must sometimes get away from the Authorized Version, if for no other reason, simply *because* it is so beautiful and so solemn. Beauty exalts, but beauty also lulls. Early associations endear but they also confuse. Through that beautiful solemnity the transporting or horrifying realities of which the book tells may come to us blunted and disarmed and we may only sigh with tranquil veneration when we ought to be burning with shame or

[1] 1 Corinthians 4:4.

87

struck dumb with terror or carried out of ourselves by ravishing hopes and adorations. Does the word "scourged"[1] really come home to us like "flogged"? Does "mocked him"[2] sting like "jeered at him"?

We ought therefore to welcome all new translations (when they are made by sound scholars) and most certainly those who are approaching the Bible for the first time will be wise not to begin with the Authorized Version – except perhaps for the historical books of the Old Testament where its archaisms suit the saga-like material well enough. Among modern translations those of Dr Moffatt[3] and Monsignor Knox[4] seem to me particularly good. The present volume concentrates on the Epistles and furnishes more help to the beginner: its scope is different. The preliminary abstracts to each letter will be found especially useful, and the reader who has not read the letters before might do well to begin by reading and reflecting on these abstracts at some length before he attempts to tackle the text. It would have saved me a great deal of labour if this book had come into my hands when I first seriously began to try to discover what Christianity was.

For a man who wants to make that discovery must face the Epistles. And whether we like it or not, most of them are by St Paul. He is the Christian author whom no one can by-pass.

[1] John 19:1.
[2] Matthew 27:29; Mark 15:20; Luke 22:63; 23:11, 36.
[3] James Moffatt (1870–1944), whose translation of the New Testament appeared in 1913, his translation of the Old Testament in 1924, the whole being revised in 1935.
[4] Ronald A. Knox (1888–1957) published a translation of the New Testament in 1945, and a translation of the Old Testament in 1949.

A most astonishing misconception has long dominated the modern mind on the subject of St Paul. It is to this effect: that Jesus preached a kindly and simple religion (found in the Gospels) and that St Paul afterwards corrupted it into a cruel and complicated religion (found in the Epistles). This is really quite untenable. All the most terrifying texts come from the mouth of Our Lord: all the texts on which we can base such warrant as we have for hoping that all men will be saved come from St Paul. If it could be proved that St Paul altered the teaching of his Master in any way, he altered it in exactly the opposite way to that which is popularly supposed. But there is no real evidence for a pre-Pauline doctrine different from St Paul's. The Epistles are, for the most part, the earliest Christian documents we possess. The Gospels come later. They are not "the Gospel", the statement of the Christian belief. They were written for those who had already been converted, who had already accepted "the Gospel". They leave out many of the "complications" (that is, the theology) because they are intended for readers who have already been instructed in it. In that sense the Epistles are more primitive and more central than the Gospels – though not, of course, than the great events which the Gospels recount. God's act (the Incarnation, the Crucifixion, and the Resurrection) comes first: the earliest theological analysis of it comes in the Epistles: then, when the generation who had known the Lord was dying out, the Gospels were composed to provide for believers a record of the great Act and of some of the Lord's sayings. The ordinary popular conception has put everything upside down. Nor is the cause far to seek. In the earlier history of every rebellion there is a stage at which you do not yet attack the King in person. You say, "The King is all right. It is his Ministers who are wrong. They misrepresent him and corrupt all his plans – which, I'm sure, are good plans if only the Ministers would let them take effect." And the first victory consists in beheading a few Ministers: only at a later stage do you go on and behead the King himself. In the same way, the nineteenth-century attack on St Paul was really only a stage in the revolt against Christ. Men were not ready in large numbers to attack Christ Himself. They made the normal first move – that of attacking one of His principal ministers. Everything they disliked in Christianity was therefore attributed to St Paul. It was unfortunate that their case could not impress anyone who had really read the Gospels and the Epistles with attention: but apparently few people had, and so the first victory was won. St Paul was impeached and banished and the world went on to the next step – the attack on the King Himself. But to those who wish to know what St Paul and his fellow-teachers really said the present volume will give great help.

13

Some Thoughts

(*1948*)

At first sight nothing seems more obvious than that religious persons should care for the sick; no Christian building, except perhaps a church, is more self-explanatory than a Christian hospital. Yet on further consideration the thing is really connected with the undying paradox, the blessedly two-edged character, of Christianity. And if any of us were now encountering Christianity for the first time he would be vividly aware of this paradox.

Let us suppose that such a person began by observing those Christian activities which are, in a sense, directed towards this present world. He would find that this religion had, as a mere matter of historical fact, been the agent which preserved such secular civilization as survived the fall of the Roman Empire; that to it Europe owes the salvation, in those perilous ages, of civilized agriculture, architecture, laws, and literacy itself. He would find that this same religion has always been healing the sick and caring for the poor; that it has, more than any other, blessed marriage; and that arts and philosophy tend to flourish in its neighbourhood. In a word, it is always either doing, or at least repenting with shame for not having done, all the things which secular humanitarianism enjoins. If our inquirer stopped at this point he would have no difficulty in classifying Christianity – giving it its place on a map of the "great religions". Obviously (he would say), this is one of the world-affirming religions like Confucianism or the agricultural religions of the great Mesopotamian city states.

But how if our inquirer began (as he well might) with quite a different series of Christian phenomena? He might notice that the central image in all Christian art was that of a Man slowly dying by torture; that the instrument of His torture was the world-wide symbol of the Faith; that martyrdom was almost the specifically Christian action; that our calendar was as full of fasts as of feasts; that we meditated constantly on the mortality not only of ourselves but of the whole universe; that we were bidden to entrust all our treasure to another world; and that even a certain disdain for the whole natural order (*contemptus mundi*) had sometimes been reckoned a Christian virtue. And here, once again, if he knew no more, the inquirer would find Christianity quite easy to classify; but this time he would classify it as one of the world-denying religions. It would be pigeon-holed along with Buddhism.

Either conclusion would be justified if a man had only the one or the other half of the evidence before him. It is when he puts both halves together and sees that Christianity cuts right across the classification he was attempting to make – it is then that he first knows what he is up against, and I think he will be bewildered.

Probably most of those who read this page have been Christians all their lives. If so, they may find it hard to sympathize with the bewilderment I refer to. To Christians the explanation of this two-edged character in their Faith seems obvious. They live in a graded or hierarchical universe where there is a place for everything and everything should be kept in its right place. The Supernatural is higher than the Natural, but each has its place; just as a man is higher than a dog, but a dog has its place. It is, therefore, to us not at all surprising that healing for the sick and provision for the poor should be less important than (when they are, as sometimes happens, alternative to) the salvation of souls; and yet very important. Because God created the Natural – invented it out of His love and artistry – it demands our reverence; because it is only a creature and not He, it is, from another point of view, of little account. And still more, because Nature, and especially human nature, is fallen it must be corrected and the evil within it must be mortified. But its essence is good; correction is something quite different from Manichaean repudiation or Stoic superiority. Hence, in all true Christian asceticism, that respect for the thing rejected which, I think, we never find in pagan asceticism. Marriage is good, though not for me; wine is good, though I must not drink it; feasts are good, though today we fast.

This attitude will, I think, be found to depend logically on the doctrines of the Creation and the Fall. Some hazy adumbrations of a doctrine of the Fall can be found in Paganism; but it is quite astonishing how rarely outside Christianity we find – I am not sure that we ever find – a real doctrine of Creation. In Polytheism the gods are usually the product of a universe already in existence – Keats' *Hyperion*, in spirit, if not in detail, is true enough as a picture of pagan theogony. In Pantheism the universe is never something that God made. It is an emanation, something that oozes out of Him, or an appearance, something He looks like to us but really is not, or even an attack of incurable schizophrenia from which He is unaccountably suffering. Polytheism is always, in the long run, nature worship; Pantheism always, in the long run, hostility to nature. None of these beliefs really leaves you free *both* to enjoy your breakfast *and* to mortify your inordinate appetites – much less to mortify appetites recognized as innocent at present lest they should become inordinate.

And none of them leaves anyone free to do what is being done in the Lourdes Hospital every day: to fight against death as earnestly, skilfully, and calmly as if you were a secular humanitarian while knowing all the time that death is, both for better and worse, something that the secular humanitarian has never dreamed of. The world, knowing how all our real investments are beyond the grave, might expect us to be less concerned than other people who go in for what is called Higher Thought and tell us that "death doesn't matter"; but we "are not high-minded",[1] and we follow One who stood and wept at the grave of Lazarus – not, surely, because He was grieved that Mary and Martha wept, and sorrowed for their lack of faith (though some thus interpret) but because death, the punishment of sin, is even more horrible in His eyes than in ours. The nature which He had created as God, the nature which He had assumed as Man, lay there before Him in its ignominy; a foul smell, food for worms. Though He was to revive it a

[1] Psalm 131:1.

moment later, He wept at the shame; if I may here quote a writer of my own communion, "I am not so much afraid of death as ashamed of it."[1] And that brings us again to the paradox. Of all men, we hope most of death; yet nothing will reconcile us to – well, its *unnaturalness*. We know that we were not made for it; we know how it crept into our destiny as an intruder; and we know Who has defeated it. Because Our Lord is risen we know that on one level it is an enemy already disarmed; but because we know that the natural level also is God's creation we cannot cease to fight against the death which mars it, as against all those other blemishes upon it, against pain and poverty, barbarism and ignorance. Because we love something else more than this world, we love even this world better than those who know no other.

---

[1] The reference is to Sir Thomas Browne's *Religio Medici*, First Part, Section 40, where he says "I am not so much afraid of death, as ashamed thereof".

14

The Humanitarian Theory
of Punishment

(*1949*)

In England we have lately had a controversy about
Capital Punishment. I do not know whether a murderer
is more likely to repent and make a good end on the
gallows a few weeks after his trial or in the prison
infirmary thirty years later. I do not know whether the
fear of death is an indispensable deterrent. I need not,
for the purpose of this article, decide whether it is a
morally permissible deterrent. Those are questions
which I propose to leave untouched. My subject is not
Capital Punishment in particular, but that theory of
punishment in general which the controversy showed to
be almost universal among my fellow-countrymen. It
may be called the Humanitarian theory. Those who
hold it think that it is mild and merciful. In this I believe
that they are seriously mistaken. I believe that the
"Humanity" which it claims is a dangerous illusion and
disguises the possibility of cruelty and injustice without
end. I urge a return to the traditional or Retributive
theory not solely, not even primarily, in the interests of
society, but in the interests of the criminal.

According to the Humanitarian theory, to punish a
man because he deserves it, and as much as he deserves,

is mere revenge, and, therefore, barbarous and immoral. It is maintained that the only legitimate motives for punishing are the desire to deter others by example or to mend the criminal. When this theory is combined, as frequently happens, with the belief that all crime is more or less pathological, the idea of mending tails off into that of healing or curing and punishment becomes therapeutic. Thus it appears at first sight that we have passed from the harsh and self-righteous notion of giving the wicked their deserts to the charitable and enlightened one of tending the psychologically sick. What could be more amiable? One little point which is taken for granted in this theory needs, however, to be made explicit. The things done to the criminal, even if they are called cures, will be just as compulsory as they were in the old days when we called them punishments. If a tendency to steal can be cured by psychotherapy, the thief will no doubt be forced to undergo the treatment. Otherwise, society cannot continue.

My contention is that this doctrine, merciful though it appears, really means that each one of us, from the moment he breaks the law, is deprived of the rights of a human being.

The reason is this. The Humanitarian theory removes from Punishment the concept of Desert. But the concept of Desert is the only connecting link between punishment and justice. It is only as deserved or undeserved that a sentence can be just or unjust. I do not here contend that the question "Is it deserved?" is the only one we can reasonably ask about a punishment. We may very properly ask whether it is likely to deter others and to reform the criminal. But neither of these two last questions is a question about justice. There is no sense in talking about a "just deterrent" or a "just cure". We demand of a deterrent not whether it is just but whether it will deter. We demand of a cure not whether it is just but whether it succeeds. Thus when we cease to consider what the criminal deserves and consider only what will cure him or deter others, we have tacitly removed him from the sphere of justice altogether; instead of a person, a subject of rights, we now have a mere object, a patient, a "case".

The distinction will become clearer if we ask who will be qualified to determine sentences when sentences are no longer held to derive their propriety from the criminal's deservings. On the old view the problem of fixing the right sentence was a moral problem. Accordingly, the judge who did it was a person trained in jurisprudence; trained, that is, in a science which deals with rights and duties, and which, in origin at least, was consciously accepting guidance from the Law of Nature, and from Scripture. We must admit that in the actual penal code of most countries at most times these high originals were so much modified by local custom, class interests, and utilitarian concessions, as to be very imperfectly recognizable. But the code was never in principle, and not always in fact, beyond the control of the conscience of the society. And when (say, in eighteenth-century England) actual punishments conflicted too violently with the moral sense of the community, juries refused to convict and reform was finally brought about. This was possible because, so long as we are thinking in terms of Desert, the propriety of the penal code, being a moral question, is a question on which every man has the right to an opinion, not because he follows this or that profession, but because he is simply a man, a rational animal enjoying the Natural Light. But all this is changed when we drop the concept of Desert. The only two questions we may now ask about a punishment are whether it deters and whether it cures. But these are not questions on which anyone is entitled to have an opinion simply because he is a man. He is not entitled to an opinion even if, in addition to being a man, he should happen also to be a jurist, a Christian, and a moral theologian. For they are not questions about principle but about matter of fact; and for such *cuiquam in sua arte credendum*.[1] Only the expert "penologist" (let barbarous things have barbarous names), in the light of previous experiment, can tell us what is likely to deter: only the psychotherapist can tell us what is likely to cure. It will be in vain for the rest of us, speaking simply as men, to say, "but this punishment is hideously unjust, hideously disproportionate to the criminal's deserts". The experts with perfect logic will reply, "But nobody was talking about deserts. No one was talking about *punishment* in your archaic vindictive sense of the word. Here are the statistics proving that this treatment deters. Here are the statistics proving that this other treatment cures. What is your trouble?"

The Humanitarian theory, then, removes sentences from the hands of jurists whom the public conscience is entitled to criticize and places them in the hands of technical experts whose special sciences do not even employ such categories as rights or justice. It might be argued that since this transference results from an

[1] We must believe the expert in his own field.

abandonment of the old idea of punishment, and, therefore, of all vindictive motives, it will be safe to leave our criminals in such hands. I will not pause to comment on the simple-minded view of fallen human nature which such a belief implies. Let us rather remember that the "cure" of criminals is to be compulsory; and let us then watch how the theory actually works in the mind of the Humanitarian. The immediate starting point of this article was a letter I read in one of our Leftist weeklies. The author was pleading that a certain sin, now treated by our laws as a crime, should henceforward be treated as a disease. And he complained that under the present system the offender, after a term in gaol, was simply let out to return to his original environment where he would probably relapse. What he complained of was not the shutting up but the letting out. On his remedial view of punishment the offender should, of course, be detained until he was cured. And of course the official straighteners are the only people who can say when that is. The first result of the Humanitarian theory is, therefore, to substitute for a definite sentence (reflecting to some extent the community's moral judgement on the degree of ill-desert involved) an indefinite sentence terminable only by the word of those experts – and they are not experts in moral theology nor even in the Law of Nature – who inflict it. Which of us, if he stood in the dock, would not prefer to be tried by the old system?

It may be said that by the continued use of the word punishment and the use of the verb "inflict" I am misrepresenting Humanitarians. They are not punishing, not inflicting, only healing. But do not let us be deceived by a name. To be taken without consent from my home and friends; to lose my liberty; to undergo all those assaults on my personality which modern psychotherapy knows how to deliver; to be re-made after some pattern of "normality" hatched in a Viennese laboratory to which I never professed allegiance; to know that this process will never end until either my captors have succeeded or I have grown wise enough to cheat them with apparent success – who cares whether this is called Punishment or not? That it includes most of the elements for which any punishment is feared – shame, exile, bondage, and years eaten by the locust – is obvious. Only enormous ill-desert could justify it; but ill-desert is the very conception which the Humanitarian theory has thrown overboard.

If we turn from the curative to the deterrent justification of punishment we shall find the new theory even more alarming. When you punish a man *in terrorem*,[1] make of him an "example" to others, you are admittedly using him as a means to an end; someone else's end. This, in itself, would be a very wicked thing to do. On the classical theory of Punishment it was of course justified on the ground that the man deserved it. That was assumed to be established before any question of "making him an example" arose. You then, as the saying is, killed two birds with one stone; in the process of giving him what he deserved you set an example to others. But take away desert and the whole morality of the punishment disappears. Why, in Heaven's name, am I to be sacrificed to the good of society in this way? – unless, of course, I deserve it.

---

[1] To cause terror.

But that is not the worst. If the justification of exemplary punishment is not to be based on desert but solely on its efficacy as a deterrent, it is not absolutely necessary that the man we punish should even have committed the crime. The deterrent effect demands that the public should draw the moral, "If we do such an act we shall suffer like that man." The punishment of a man actually guilty whom the public think innocent will not have the desired effect; the punishment of a man actually innocent will, provided the public think him guilty. But every modern State has powers which make it easy to fake a trial. When a victim is urgently needed for exemplary purposes and a guilty victim cannot be found, all the purposes of deterrence will be equally served by the punishment (call it "cure" if you prefer) of an innocent victim, provided that the public can be cheated into thinking him guilty. It is no use to ask me why I assume that our rulers will be so wicked. The punishment of an innocent, that is, an undeserving, man is wicked only if we grant the traditional view that righteous punishment means deserved punishment. Once we have abandoned that criterion, all punishments have to be justified, if at all, on other grounds that have nothing to do with desert. Where the punishment of the innocent can be justified on those grounds (and it could in some cases be justified as a deterrent) it will be no less moral than any other punishment. Any distaste for it on the part of a Humanitarian will be merely a hang-over from the Retributive theory.

It is, indeed, important to notice that my argument so far supposes no evil intentions on the part of the

Humanitarian and considers only what is involved in the logic of his position. My contention is that good men (not bad men) consistently acting upon that position would act as cruelly and unjustly as the greatest tyrants. They might in some respects act even worse. Of all tyrannies a tyranny sincerely exercised for the good of its victims may be the most oppressive. It may be better to live under robber barons than under omnipotent moral busybodies. The robber baron's cruelty may sometimes sleep, his cupidity may at some point be satiated; but those who torment us for our own good will torment us without end for they do so with the approval of their own conscience. They may be more likely to go to Heaven yet at the same time likelier to make a Hell on earth. Their very kindness stings with intolerable insult. To be "cured" against one's will and cured of states which we may not regard as disease is to be put on a level with those who have not yet reached the age of reason or those who never will; to be classed with infants, imbeciles, and domestic animals. But to be punished, however severely, because we have deserved it, because we "ought to have known better", is to be treated as a human person made in God's image.

In reality, however, we must face the possibility of bad rulers armed with a Humanitarian theory of punishment. A great many popular blue-prints for a Christian society are merely what the Elizabethans called "eggs in moonshine" because they assume that the whole society is Christian or that the Christians are in control. This is not so in most contemporary States. Even if it were, our rulers would still be fallen men, and, therefore, neither very wise nor very good. As it is, they will usually be unbelievers. And since wisdom and virtue are not the only or the commonest qualifications for a place in the government, they will not often be even the best unbelievers. The practical problem of Christian politics is not that of drawing up schemes for a Christian society, but that of living as innocently as we can with unbelieving fellow-subjects under unbelieving rulers who will never be perfectly wise and good and who will sometimes be very wicked and very foolish. And when they are wicked the Humanitarian theory of punishment will put in their hands a finer instrument of tyranny than wickedness ever had before. For if crime and disease are to be regarded as the same thing, it follows that any state of mind which our masters choose to call "disease" can be treated as crime; and compulsorily cured. It will be vain to plead that states of mind which displease government need not always involve moral turpitude and do not therefore always deserve forfeiture of liberty. For our masters will not be using the concepts of Desert and Punishment but those of disease and cure. We know that one school of psychology already regards religion as a neurosis. When this particular neurosis becomes inconvenient to government, what is to hinder government from proceeding to "cure" it? Such "cure" will, of course, be compulsory; but under the Humanitarian theory it will not be called by the shocking name of Persecution. No one will blame us for being Christian, no one will hate us, no one will revile us. The new Nero will approach us with the silky manners of a doctor, and though all will be in fact as compulsory as the *tunica molesta* or Smithfield or Tyburn, all will go on within the unemotional therapeutic sphere where words like "right" and "wrong" or "freedom" and "slavery" are never heard. And thus when the command is given, every prominent Christian in the land may vanish overnight into Institutions for the Treatment of the Ideologically Unsound, and it will rest with the expert gaolers to say when (if ever) they are to re-emerge. But it will not be persecution. Even if the treatment is painful, even if it is life-long, even if it is fatal, that will be only a regrettable accident; the intention was purely therapeutic. Even in ordinary medicine there were painful operations and fatal operations: so in this. But because they are "treatment", not punishment, they can be criticized only by fellow-experts and on technical grounds, never by men as men and on grounds of justice.

This is why I think it essential to oppose the Humanitarian theory of punishment, root and branch, wherever we encounter it. It carries on its front a semblance of mercy which is wholly false. That is how it can deceive men of good will. The error began, perhaps, with Shelley's statement that the distinction between mercy and justice was invented in the courts of tyrants. It sounds noble, and was indeed the error of a noble mind. But the distinction is essential. The older view was that mercy "tempered" justice, or (on the highest level of all) that mercy and justice had met and kissed. The essential act of mercy was to pardon; and pardon in its very essence involves the recognition of guilt and ill-desert in the recipient. If crime is only a disease which needs cure, not sin which deserves punishment, it cannot be pardoned. How can you pardon a man for having a gumboil or a club foot? But the Humanitarian theory wants simply to abolish Justice and substitute Mercy for it. This means that you start being "kind" to people before you have considered their rights, and then force upon them supposed kindnesses which no one but you will recognize as kindnesses and which the recipient will feel as abominable cruelties. You have overshot the mark. Mercy, detached from Justice, grows unmerciful. That is the important paradox. As there are plants which will flourish only in mountain soil, so it appears that Mercy will flower only when it grows in the crannies of the rock of Justice: transplanted to the Marshlands of mere Humanitarianism, it becomes a man-eating weed, all the more dangerous because it is still called by the same name as the mountain variety. But we ought long ago to have learned our lesson. We should be too old now to be deceived by those humane pretensions which have served to usher in every cruelty of the revolutionary period in which we live. These are the "precious balms" which will "break our heads".[1]

There is a fine sentence in Bunyan: "It came burning hot into my mind, whatever he said, and however he flattered, when he got me home to his House, he would sell me for a Slave."[2] There is a fine couplet, too, in John Ball:

> Be war or ye be wo;
> Knoweth your freed from your foo.[3]

[1] Psalm 141:5.
[2] *The Pilgrim's Progress*, ed. James Blanton Wharey, second edition revised by Roger Sharrock, Oxford English Texts (Oxford, 1960), Part I, p. 70.
[3] "John Ball's Letter to the Peasants of Essex, 1381", lines 11–12, found in *Fourteenth Century Verse and Prose*, ed. Kenneth Sisam (Oxford, 1921), p. 161.

The Humanitarian Theory of Punishment

PART II
On Punishment: A Reply
by C. S. Lewis
(1954)

I have to thank the Editor for this opportunity of replying to two most interesting critiques of my article on the Humanitarian Theory of Punishment, one by Professor J.J.C. Smart[1] and the other by Drs N. Morris and D. Buckle.[2]

Professor Smart makes a distinction between questions of the First and of the Second Order. "First" are questions like "Ought I to return this book?"; "Second", like "Is promise-making a good institution?" He claims that these two Orders of question require different methods of treatment. The first can be answered by Intuition (in the sense which moral philosophers sometimes give that word). We "see" what is "right" at once, because the proposed action falls under a rule. But second-order questions can be answered only on "utilitarian" principles. Since "right" means "agreeable to the rules" it is senseless to ask if the rules themselves are "right"; we can only ask if they are useful. A parallel would be this: granted a fixed spelling we may ask whether a word is spelled correctly, but cannot ask whether the spelling system is correct, only if it is consistent or convenient. Or again, a form may be grammatically right, but the grammar of a whole language cannot be right or wrong.

[1] "Comment: The Humanitarian Theory of Punishment", *Res Judicatae*, Vol. VI (February 1954), pp. 368–71.
[2] "Reply to C.S. Lewis", *Res Judicatae*, Vol. VI (June 1953), pp. 231–7.

Professor Smart is here, of course, treating in a new way a very ancient distinction. It was realized by all the thinkers of the past that you could consider either (*a*) Whether an act was "just" in the sense of conforming to a law or custom, or (*b*) Whether a law or custom was itself "just". To the ancient and medievals, however, the distinction was one between (*a*) Justice by law or convention, *nomo* (*i*) and (*b*) Justice "simply" or "by nature", *haplôs* or *physei*, or between (*a*) Positive Law, and (*b*) Natural Law. Both inquiries were about justice, but the distinction between them was acknowledged. The novelty of Professor Smart's system consists in confining the concept of justice to the first-order questions.

It is claimed that the new system (1) avoids a *petitio* inherent in any appeal to the Law of Nature or the "simply" just; for "to say that this is the Law of Nature is only to say that this is the rule we should adopt"; and (2) gets rid of dogmatic subjectivism. For the idea of desert in my article may be only "Lewis's personal preference".

I am not convinced, however, that Professor Smart's system does avoid these inconveniences.

Those rules are to be accepted which are useful to the community, utility being (I think) what will make that community "happier".[1] Does this mean that the happiness of the community is to be pursued *at all costs*, or only to be pursued in so far as this pursuit is compatible with certain degrees of mercy, human dignity and veracity? (I must not add "of justice" because, in Professor Smart's view, the rules themselves cannot be either just or unjust.) If we take the second alternative, if we admit that there are some things, or even any one

[1] See the penultimate paragraph of Professor Smart's article.

thing, which a community ought not to do however much it will increase its happiness, then we have really given up the position. We are now judging the useful by some other standard (whether we call it Conscience, or Practical Reason, or Law of Nature or Personal Preference). Suppose then, we take the first alternative: the happiness of the community is to be pursued at all costs. In certain circumstances the costs may be very heavy. In war, in some not improbable future when the world's food runs short, during some threat of revolution, very shocking things may be likely to make the community happier or to preserve its existence. We cannot be sure that frame-ups, witch-hunts, even cannibalism, would never be in this sense "useful". Let us suppose (what, I am very sure, is false) that Professor Smart is prepared to go the whole hog. It then remains to ask him why he does so or why he thinks we should agree with him. He of all men cannot reply that *salus populi suprema lex*[1] is the Law of Nature; firstly, because we others know that "the people should be preserved" is not the Law of Nature but only one clause in that Law. What then could a pursuit of the community's happiness at all costs be based on if not on Professor Smart's "personal preference"? The real difference between him and me would then be simply that we have different desires. Or, rather, that I have one more desire than he. For, like him, I desire the continuance and happiness of my country (and species),[2] but

---

[1] The safety of the people is the highest law. Cicero, *De Legibus*, Book III, part iii, section 8.

[2] I am not sure whether for Professor Smart the "community" means the nation or the species. If the former, difficulties arise about international morality, in discussing which I think Professor Smart would have to come to the species sooner or later.

then I also desire that they should be people of a certain sort, behaving in a certain way. The second desire is the stronger of the two. If I cannot have both, I had rather that the human race, having a certain quality in their lives, should continue for only a few centuries than that, losing freedom, friendship, dignity and mercy, and learning to be quite content without them, they should continue for millions of millennia. If it is merely a matter of wishes, there is really no further question for discussion. Lots of people feel like me, and lots feel the other way. I believe that it is in our age being decided which kind of men will win.

And that is why, if I may say so without discourtesy, Professor Smart and I both matter so little compared with Drs Morris and Buckle. We are only dons; they are criminologists, a lawyer and a psychiatrist respectively. And the only thing which leads me so far off my own beat as to write about "Penology" at all is my intense anxiety as to which side in this immensely important conflict will have the Law for its ally. This leads me to the only serious disagreement between my two critics and myself.

Other disagreements there are, but they mainly turn on misunderstandings for which I am probably to blame. Thus:

(1) There was certainly too little, if there was anything, in my article about the protection of the community. I am afraid I took it for granted. But the distinction in my mind would not be, as my critics suppose [Morris and Buckle, p. 232], one between "subsidiary" and "vital" elements in punishment. I call the act of taking a packet of cigarettes off a counter and slipping it

110

into one's pocket "purchase" or "theft" according as one does or does not pay for it. This does not mean that I consider the taking away of the goods as "subsidiary" in an act of purchase. It means that what legitimizes it, what makes it purchase at all, is the paying. I call the sexual act chaste or unchaste according as the parties are or are not married to one another. This does not mean that I consider it as "subsidiary" to marriage, but that what legitimizes it, what makes it a specimen of conjugal behaviour at all, is marriage. In the same way, I am ready to make both the protection of society and the "cure" of the criminal as important as you please in punishment, but only on a certain condition; namely, that the initial act of thus interfering with a man's liberty be justified on grounds of desert. Like payment in purchase, or marriage as regards the sexual act, it is this, and (I believe) this alone, which legitimizes our proceeding and makes it an instance of punishment at all, instead of an instance of tyranny – or, perhaps, of war.

(2) I agree about criminal *children* [see Morris and Buckle, p. 234]. There has been progress in this matter. Very primitive societies will "try" and "punish" an axe or a spear in cases of unintentional homicide. Somewhere (I think, in the Empire) during the later Middle Ages a pig was solemnly tried for murder. Till quite recently, we may (I don't know) have tried children as if they had adult responsibility. These things have rightly been abolished. But the whole question is whether you want the process to be carried further: whether you want us all to be simultaneously deprived of the protection and released from the responsibilities of adult citizenship and reduced to the level of the child, the pig and the axe.

I don't want this because I don't think there are in fact any people who stand to the rest of us as adult to child, man to beast or animate to inanimate.[1] I think the laws which laid down a "desertless" theory of punishment would in reality be made and administered by people just like the rest of us.

But the real disagreement is this. Drs Morris and Buckle, fully alive to dangers of the sort I dread and reprobating them no less than I, believe that we have a safeguard. It lies in the Courts, in their incorruptible judges, their excellent techniques and "the controls of natural justice which the law has built up" [p. 233]. Yes; if the whole tradition of natural justice which the law has for so long incorporated, will survive the completion of that change in our attitude to punishment which we are now discussing. But that for me is precisely the question. Our Courts, I agree, "have traditionally represented the common man and the common man's view of morality" [p. 233]. It is true that we must extend the term "common man" to cover Locke, Grotius, Hooker, Poynet, Aquinas, Justinian, the Stoics and Aristotle, but I have no objection to that; in one most important, and to me glorious, sense they were all common men.[2] But that whole tradition is tied up with ideas of free will, responsibility, rights and the law of nature. Can it survive in Courts whose penal practice daily subordinates "desert" to therapy and the protection of

[1] This is really the same objection as that which I would make to Aristotle's theory of slavery (*Politics* 1254A *et seq.*). We can all recognize the "natural" slaves (I am perhaps one myself) but where are the "natural" masters?

[2] See also Lewis: *The Abolition of Man* (London, 1943), especially the Appendix.

society? Can the Law assume one philosophy in practice and continue to enjoy the safeguards of a different philosophy?

I write as the son of one lawyer and the life-long friend of another, to two criminologists one of whom is a lawyer. I believe an approximation between their view and mine is not to be despaired of, for we have the same ends at heart. I wish society to be protected and I should be very glad if all punishments were also cures. All I plead for is the *prior* condition of ill-desert; loss of liberty justified on retributive grounds *before* we begin considering the other factors. After that, as you please. Till that, there is really no question of "punishment". We are not such poltroons that we want to be protected unconditionally, though when a man has deserved punishment we shall very properly look to our protection in devising it. We are not such busybodies that we want to improve all our neighbours by force; but when one of our neighbours has justly forfeited his right not to be interfered with, we shall charitably try to make his punishment improve him. But we will not presume to teach him (who, after all, are we?) till he has merited that we should "larn him". Will Dr Morris and Dr Buckle come so far to meet me as that? On their decision and on that of others in similar important offices, depends, I believe, the continued dignity and beneficence of that great discipline the Law, but also much more. For, if I am not deceived, we are all at this moment helping to decide whether humanity shall retain all that has hitherto made humanity worth preserving, or whether we must slide down into the sub-humanity imagined by Mr Aldous Huxley and George Orwell and partially realized in

Hitler's Germany. For the extermination of the Jews really would have been "useful" if the racial theories had been correct; there is no foretelling what may come to seem, or even to be, "useful", and "necessity" was always "the tyrant's plea".

15

Xmas and Christmas
A Lost Chapter from Herodotus
(*1954*)

And beyond this there lies in the ocean, turned towards the west and north, the island of Niatirb which Hecataeus indeed declares to be the same size and shape as Sicily, but it is larger, though in calling it triangular a man would not miss the mark. It is densely inhabited by men who wear clothes not very different from the other barbarians who occupy the north-western parts of Europe though they do not agree with them in language. These islanders, surpassing all the men of whom we know in patience and endurance, use the following customs.

In the middle of winter when fogs and rains most abound they have a great festival which they call Exmas, and for fifty days they prepare for it in the fashion I shall describe. First of all, every citizen is obliged to send to each of his friends and relations a square piece of hard paper stamped with a picture, which in their speech is called an Exmas-card. But the pictures represent birds sitting on branches, or trees with a dark green prickly leaf, or else men in such garments as the Niatirbians believe that their ancestors wore two hundred years ago riding in coaches such as their ancestors used, or houses with snow on their roofs. And the Niatirbians are unwilling to say what these pictures have to do with the festival, guarding (as I suppose) some sacred mystery. And because all men must send these cards the market-place is filled with the crowd of those buying them, so that there is great labour and weariness.

But having bought as many as they suppose to be sufficient, they return to their houses and find there the like cards which others have sent to them. And when they find cards from any to whom they also have sent cards, they throw them away and give thanks to the gods that this labour at least is over for another year. But when they find cards from any to whom they have not sent, then they beat their breasts and wail and utter curses against the sender; and, having sufficiently lamented their misfortune, they put on their boots again and go out into the fog and rain and buy a card for him also. And let this account suffice about Exmas-cards.

They also send gifts to one another, suffering the same things about the gifts as about the cards, or even worse. For every citizen has to guess the value of the gift which every friend will send to him so that he may send one of equal value, whether he can afford it or not. And they buy as gifts for one another such things as no man ever bought for himself. For the sellers, understanding the custom, put forth all kinds of trumpery, and whatever, being useless and ridiculous, they have been unable to sell throughout the year they now sell as an Exmas gift. And though the Niatirbians profess themselves to lack sufficient necessary things, such as metal, leather, wood and paper, yet an incredible quantity of these things is wasted every year, being made into the gifts.

116

But during these fifty days the oldest, poorest and most miserable of the citizens put on false beards and red robes and walk about the market-place; being disguised (in my opinion) as *Cronos*. And the sellers of gifts no less than the purchasers become pale and weary, because of the crowds and the fog, so that any man who came into a Niatirbian city at this season would think some great public calamity had fallen on Niatirb. This fifty days of preparation is called in their barbarian speech the Exmas *Rush*.

But when the day of the festival comes, then most of the citizens, being exhausted with the *Rush*, lie in bed till noon. But in the evening they eat five times as much supper as on other days and, crowning themselves with crowns of paper, they become intoxicated. And on the day after Exmas they are very grave, being internally disordered by the supper and the drinking and reckoning how much they have spent on gifts and on the wine. For wine is so dear among the Niatirbians that a man must swallow the worth of a talent before he is well intoxicated.

Such, then, are their customs about the Exmas. But the few among the Niatirbians have also a festival, separate and to themselves, called Crissmas, which is on the same day as Exmas. And those who keep Crissmas, doing the opposite to the majority of the Niatirbians, rise early on that day with shining faces and go before sunrise to certain temples where they partake of a sacred feast. And in most of the temples they set out images of a fair woman with a new-born Child on her knees and certain animals and shepherds adoring the Child. (The reason of these images is given in a certain sacred story which I know but do not repeat.)

117

But I myself conversed with a priest in one of these temples and asked him why they kept Crissmas on the same day as Exmas; for it appeared to me inconvenient. But the priest replied, It is not lawful, O Stranger, for us to change the date of Crissmas, but would that Zeus would put it into the minds of the Niatirbians to keep Exmas at some other time or not to keep it at all. For Exmas and the *Rush* distract the minds even of the few from sacred things. And we indeed are glad that men should make merry at Crissmas; but in Exmas there is no merriment left. And when I asked him why they endured the *Rush*, he replied, It is, O Stranger, a *racket*; using (as I suppose) the words of some oracle and speaking unintelligibly to me (for a *racket* is an instrument which the barbarians use in a game called *tennis*).

But what Hecataeus says, that Exmas and Crissmas are the same, is not credible. For first, the pictures which are stamped on the Exmas-cards have nothing to do with the sacred story which the priests tell about Crissmas. And secondly, the most part of the Niatirbians, not believing the religion of the few, nevertheless send the gifts and cards and participate in the *Rush* and drink, wearing paper caps. But it is not likely that men, even being barbarians, should suffer so many and great things in honour of a god they do not believe in. And now, enough about Niatirb.

16

Revival or Decay?

(*1958*)

"But would you deny", said the Headmaster, "that there is, here in the West, a great, even growing, interest in religion?"

It is not the sort of question I find easy to answer. *Great* and *growing* would seem to involve statistics, and I had no statistics. I supposed there was a fairly widespread interest. But I didn't feel sure the Headmaster was interpreting it correctly. In the days when most people had a religion, what he meant by "an interest in religion" could hardly have existed. For of course religious people – that is, people when they are being religious – are not "interested in religion". Men who have gods worship those gods; it is the spectators who describe this as "religion". The Maenads thought about Dionysus, not about religion. *Mutatis mutandis* this goes for Christians too. The moment a man seriously accepts a deity his interest in "religion" is at an end. He's got something else to think about. The ease with which we can now get an audience for a discussion of religion does not prove that more people are becoming religious. What it really proves is the existence of a large "floating vote". Every conversion will reduce this potential audience.

Once the climate of opinion allows such a floating

vote to form I see no reason why it should speedily diminish. Indecision, often very honest, is very natural. It would be foolish, however, not to realize that it is also no hardship. Floating is a very agreeable operation; a decision either way costs something. Real Christianity and consistent Atheism both make demands on a man. But to admit, on occasion, and as possibilities, all the comforts of the one without its discipline – to enjoy all the liberty of the other without its philosophical and emotional abstinences – well, this may be honest, but there's no good pretending it is uncomfortable.

"And would you, further, deny", said the Headmaster, "that Christianity commands more respect in the most highly educated circles than it has done for centuries? The Intelligentsia are coming over. Look at men like Maritain, like Bergson, like –"

But I didn't feel at all happy about this. Of course the converted Intellectual is a characteristic figure of our times. But this phenomenon would be more hopeful if it had not occurred at a moment when the Intelligentsia (scientists apart) are losing all touch with, and all influence over, nearly the whole human race. Our most esteemed poets and critics are read by our most esteemed critics and poets (who don't usually like them much) and nobody else takes any notice. An increasing number of highly literate people simply ignore what the "Highbrows" are doing. It says nothing to them. The Highbrows in return ignore or insult them. Conversions from the Intelligentsia are not therefore likely to be very widely influential. They may even raise a horrid suspicion that Christianity itself has become part of the general "Highbrow racket", has been adopted, like

Surrealism and the pictures painted by chimpanzees, as one more method of "shocking the bourgeois". This would be dreadfully uncharitable, no doubt; but then the Intelligentsia have said a great many uncharitable things about the others.

"Then again," boomed the Headmaster, "even where there is, or is as yet, no explicit religion, do we not see a vast rallying to the defence of those standards which, whether recognized or not, make part of our spiritual heritage? The Western – may I not say the Christian – values . . ."

We all winced. And to me in particular there came back the memory of a corrugated iron hut used as an R.A.F chapel – a few kneeling airmen – and a young chaplain uttering the prayer, "Teach us, O Lord, to love *the things Thou standest for.*" He was perfectly sincere, and I willingly believe that the *things* in question included something more and better than "the Western values", whatever those may be. And yet . . . his words seemed to me to imply a point of view incompatible with Christianity or indeed with any serious Theism whatever. God is not, for it, the goal or end. He is (and how fortunate!) enlightened; has, or "stands for", the right ideals. He is valued for that reason. He ranks, admittedly, as a leader. But of course a leader leads to something beyond himself. That something else is the real goal. This is miles away from "Thou hast made us for Thyself and our heart has no rest till it comes to Thee." The Maenads were more religious.

"And the substitutes for religion are being discredited," continued the Headmaster. "Science has become more a bogy than a god. The Marxist heaven on earth –"

And only the other day a lady told me that a girl to whom she had mentioned death replied, "Oh, but by the time I'm *that* age Science will have done something about it." And then I remembered how often, in disputing before simple audiences, I had found the assured belief that whatever was wrong with man would in the long run (and not so very long a run either) be put right by "Education". And that led me to think of all the "approaches" to "religion" I actually meet. An anonymous postcard tells me that I ought to be flogged at the cart's tail for professing to believe in the Virgin Birth. A distinguished literary atheist to whom I am introduced mutters, looks away, and walks swiftly to the far end of the room. An unknown American writes to ask me whether Elijah's fiery chariot was really a Flying Saucer. I encounter Theosophists, British Israelites, Spiritualists, Pantheists. Why do people like the Headmaster always talk about "religion"? Why not religions? We seethe with religions. Christianity, I am pleased to note, is one of them. I get letters from saints, who have no notion they are any such thing, showing in every line radiant faith, joy, humility, and even humour, in appalling suffering. I get others from converts who want to apologize for some small incivility they committed against me in print years ago.

These bits and pieces are all "the West" I really know at first hand. They escape the Headmaster's treatment. He speaks from books and articles. The real sanctities, hatreds and lunacies which surround us are hardly represented there. Still less, the great negative factor. It is something more than ignorance as he would understand the word. Most people's thinking lacks a dimension which he takes for granted. Two instances may make the distinction clear. Once, after I had said something on the air about Natural Law, an old Colonel (obviously *anima candida*)[1] wrote to say that this had interested him very much and could I just tell him of "some handy little *brochure* which dealt with the subject fully". That is ignorance, striking only in degree. Here is the other. A vet, a workman, and I were wearily stumbling about on a Home Guard patrol in the small hours. The vet and I got talking about the causes of wars and arrived at the conclusion that we must expect them to recur. "But – but – but –" gasped the workman. There was a moment's silence, and he broke out, "But then what's the good of the ruddy world going on?" I got a very clear impression of what was happening. For the first time in his life a really ultimate question was before him. The sort of thing we have been considering all our lives – the meaning of existence – had just broken upon him. It was a wholly new dimension.

Is there a homogeneous "West"? I doubt it. Everything that can go on is going on all round us. Religions buzz about us like bees. A serious sex worship – quite different from the cheery lechery endemic in our species – is one of them. Traces of embryonic religions occur in science fiction. Meanwhile, as always, the Christian way too is followed. But nowadays, when it is not followed, it need not be feigned. That fact covers a good deal of what is called the decay of religion. Apart from that, is the present so very different from other ages or "the West" from anywhere else?

[1] A candid, frank soul.

17

Before We Can Communicate

(*1961*)

I have been asked to write about "the problem of communication"; by which my inquirer meant "communication under modern conditions between Christians and the outer world". And, as usually happens to me when I am questioned, I feel a little embarrassed by the simplicity and unexcitingness of the answer I want to give. I feel that what I have to say is on a cruder and lower level than was hoped for.

My ideas about "communication" are purely empirical, and two anecdotes (both strictly true) will illustrate the sort of experience on which they are based.

1. The old Prayer Book prayed that the magistrates might "truly and indifferently administer justice". Then the revisers thought they would make this easier by altering *indifferently* to *impartially*. A country clergyman of my acquaintance asked his sexton what he thought *indifferently* meant, and got the correct answer, "It means making no difference between one chap and another." "And what", continued the parson, "do you think *impartially* means?" "Ah," said the sexton after a pause, "I wouldn't know *that*."

Everyone sees what the revisers had in mind. They

were afraid that the "man in the pew" would take *in-differently* to mean, as it often does, "carelessly", without concern. They knew that this error would not be made by highly educated people, but they thought it would be made by everyone else. The sexton's reply, however, reveals that it will not be made by the least educated class of all. It will be made only by those who are educationally in the middle; those whose language is fashionable (our elders would have said "polite") without being scholarly. The highest and lowest classes are both equally safe from it; and *impartially*, which guards the "middle" churchgoers from misunderstanding, is meaningless to the simple.

2. During the war I got into a discussion with a working man about the Devil. He said he believed in a Devil, but "not a personal Devil". As the discussion proceeded it grew more and more perplexing to both parties. It became clear that we were somehow at cross-purposes. Then, suddenly and almost by accident, I discovered what was wrong. It became obvious that he had, all along, been meaning by the word *personal* nothing more or less or other than *corporeal*. He was a very intelligent man, and, once this discovery had been made, there was no difficulty. Apparently we had not really disagreed about anything: the difference between us was merely one of vocabulary. It set me wondering how many of the thousands of people who say they "believe in God but not in a personal God" are really trying to tell us no more than that they are not, in the strict sense, *anthropomorphists* and are, in fact, asserting, on this point, their perfect orthodoxy.

Where the revisers of the Prayer Book and I both

went wrong was this. We both had *a priori* notions of what simple people mean by words. I assumed that the workman's usage was the same as my own. The revisers, more subtly but not more correctly, assumed that all would know the sense of *indifferently* which they were guarding against when they amended it. But apparently we must not decide *a priori* what other people mean by English words any more than what Frenchmen mean by French words. We must be wholly empirical. We must listen, and note, and memorize. And of course we must set aside every trace of snobbery or pedantry about "right" or "wrong" usages.

Now this is, I feel, very humdrum and workaday. When one wants to discuss the problem of communication on a grand, philosophical level, when one wants to talk about conflicts of *Weltanschauung* and the predicament of modern, or urban, or crisis consciousness, it is chilling to be told that the first step is simply linguistic in the crudest sense. But it is.

What we want to see in every ordination exam is a compulsory paper on (simply) translation; a passage from some theological work to be turned into plain vernacular English. Just turned: not adorned, nor diluted, nor made "matey". The exercise is very like doing Latin prose. Instead of saying, "How would Cicero have said that?" you have to ask yourself, "How would my scout or bedmaker have said that?"

You will at once find that this labour has two useful by-products.

1. In the very process of eliminating from your matter all that is technical, learned or allusive, you will discover, perhaps for the first time, the true value of

learned language: namely, brevity. It can say in ten words what popular speech can hardly get into a hundred. Your popularization of the passage set will have to be very much longer than the original. And this we must just put up with.

2. You will also discover – at least I, a copious "translator", think I have discovered – just how much you yourself have, up to that moment, been understanding the language which you are now trying to translate. Again and again I have been most usefully humiliated in this way. One holds, or thinks one holds, a particular view, say, of the Atonement or Orders or Inspiration. And you can go on for years discussing and defending it to others *of your own sort*. New refinements can be introduced to meet its critics; brilliant metaphors can seem to illuminate its obscurities; comparisons with other views, "placings" of it, are somehow felt to establish its position in a sort of aristocracy of ideas. For the others are all talking the same language and all move in the same world of discourse. All seems well. Then turn and try to expound this same view to an intelligent mechanic or a sincerely inquisitive, but superficially quite irreverent, schoolboy. Some question of shattering crudity (it would never be asked in learned circles) will be shot at you. You are like a skilled swordsman transfixed by an opponent who wins just because he knows none of the first principles. The crude question turns out to be fatal. You have never, it now appears, really understood what you have so long maintained. You haven't really thought it out; not to the end; not to "the absolute ruddy end".

You must either give it up, or else begin it all over

again. If, given patience and ordinary skill, you cannot explain a thing to any sensible person whatever (provided he will listen), then you don't really understand it yourself. Here too it is very like doing Latin prose; the bits you can't get into Latin are usually the bits you haven't really grasped in the English.

What we need to be particularly on our guard against are precisely the vogue words, the incantatory words, of our own circle. For your generation they are, perhaps, *engagement, commitment, over against, under judgement, existential, crisis,* and *confrontation.* These are, of all expressions, the least likely to be intelligible to anyone divided from you by a school of thought, by a decade, by a social class. They are like family language, or a school slang. And our private language may delude ourselves as well as mystifying outsiders. Enchanted words seem so full of meaning, so illuminating. But we may be deceived. What we derive from them may sometimes be not so much a clear conception as a heart-warming sense of being at home and among our own sort. "We understand one another" often means "We are in sympathy". Sympathy is a good thing. It may even be in some ways a better thing than intellectual understanding. But not the same thing.